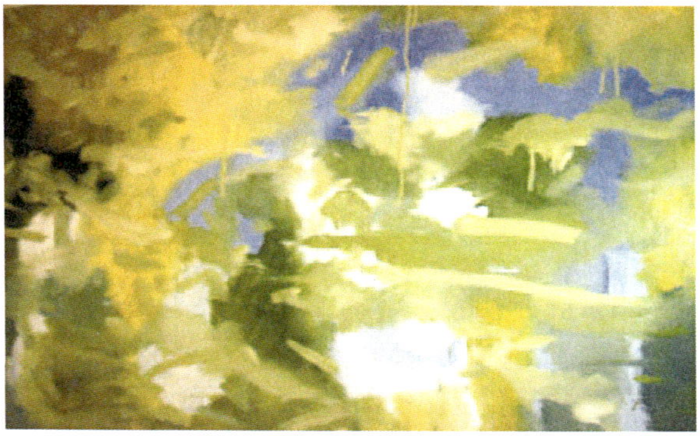

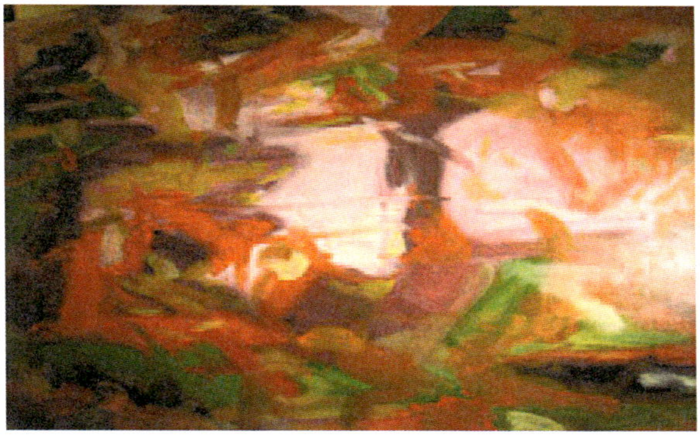

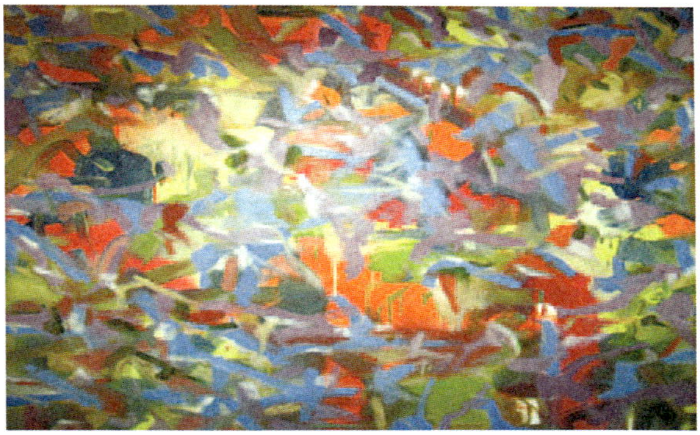

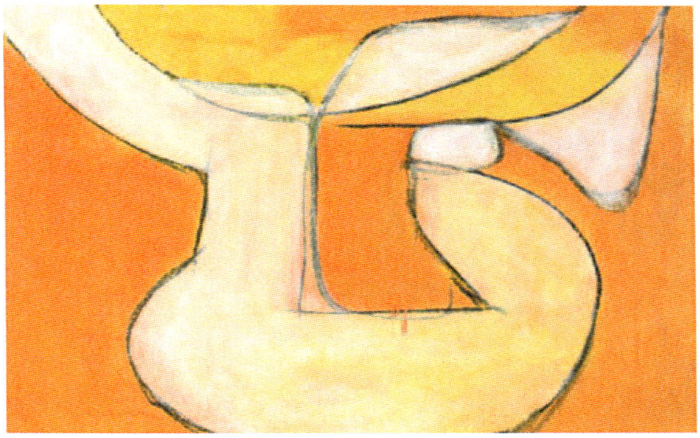

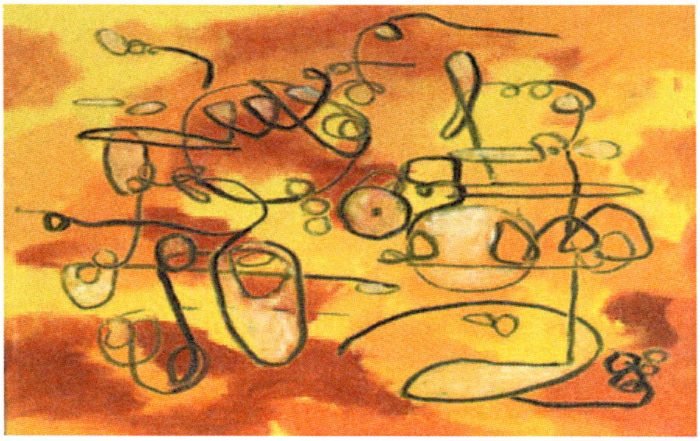

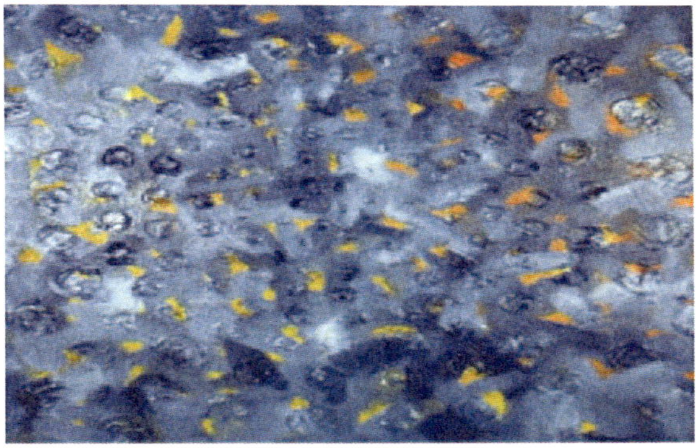

I am transforming today.
All good things are coming my way ☺

Written by Cindy Miller
http://isthatallthereisthejourneywithin.com
Read Cindy's book

Eat to be well and you'll feel swell!!!! ☺

Written by Cindy Miller
http://isthatallthereisthejourneywithin.com
Read Cindy's book

God is watching over me,
He is in all I see ☺

Written by Cindy Miller
http://isthatallthereisthejourneywithin.com
Read Cindy's book

The time is here for me to soar!
There is so much more for me to explore. ☺

Written by Cindy Miller
http://isthatallthereisthejourneywithin.com
Read Cindy's book

What is it that makes me smile?
I know I am worthwhile. ☺

Written by Cindy Miller
http://isthatallthereisthejourneywithin.com
Read Cindy's book

The day is here for me to greet.
Let there be joy in my heart with all I meet. ☺

Written by Cindy Miller
http://isthatallthereisthejourneywithin.com
Read Cindy's book

3

My heart skips a beat when I am tense,
so I need to let down my defense. ☺

Written by Cindy Miller
http://isthatallthereisthejourneywithin.com
Read Cindy's book

I have nothing to fear
for the Lord my God is always near. ☺

Written by Cindy Miller
http://isthatallthereisthejourneywithin.com
Read Cindy's book

What I eat this blessed day will build
and shape my body each and every day. ☺

Written by Cindy Miller
http://isthatallthereisthejourneywithin.com
Read Cindy's book

Exercise doesn't have to be hard
it just means to move, if only a yard. ☺

Written by Cindy Miller
http://isthatallthereisthejourneywithin.com
Read Cindy's book

Love is around me wherever I go.
I feel it and let it show. ☺

Written by Cindy Miller
http://isthatallthereisthejourneywithin.com
Read Cindy's book

Be enthusiastic about life. Greet each day with enthusiasm as you relish in God's love.

Written by Cindy Miller
http://isthatallthereisthejourneywithin.com
Read Cindy's book

»»»»» Take Action «««««

These cards are designed to carry around, pin up or hand out so that they can be picked up or looked at throughout the day. I recommend you place them somewhere visible.

Pay it forward.
Pass on some cards to those you feel would appreciate the message.

Imagine

Table of Contents

Acknowledgments 10
Dedication 11
Foreword 12
Introduction 13
How To Use This Workbook 15

1. Am I Happy? _____ 17
2. That Thing Called Joy _____ 27
3. What Needs to Change? _____ 53
4. My Aspirations _____ 69
5. The Drama - Is It Holding Me Back? _____ 87
6. The People in your Life: Love, Loss, and Forgiveness 99
7. Do I Dress My Part? _____ 127
8. Not Another Workshop Or Book _____ 137
9. Prayers and Signs from God _____ 145
10. We All Have This In Common _____ 155
11. Let Go, Let In _____ 165
12. I Know Who I Am _____ 173
13. R U Changing - Transformation _____ 181

About the Author _____ *210*

Acknowledgments

Interior formatting by: Eric Mesh and Richard Teasdale

Template design by Richard Teasdale

Book cover art and card art by: Steven Miller   www.stevenwmiller.com

Design assistance by Diane Cashman

Formatting and Graphics: Richard Teasdale, Eric Mesh

Editing: John Bobowski, Jeanne Foege, Richard Teasdale

Girl image Artist: Steven Miller

Computer Assistance: Henry Hull

This project could not have been completed without the help of the above team. They have been amazing!

Dedication

> *Here's to looking at you*
>
> *You are the mirror*
>
> *In the mirror is your reflection*
>
> *A reflection of God's pure love*
>
> *May you see, feel and know you are loved*
>
> *Be willing to cast out all fear*
>
> *You are the perfect child of the universe*
>
> *Now revel in your perfection*
>
> *and your life!*
>
> written by Cindy Miller

Foreword

Cindy Miller is an amazing woman!

We have been friends since 2005 and while I don't pretend to know all of the nitty-gritty details of her life, what I do know about her is worth sharing.

Cindy comes from a broken home, had an alcoholic and abusive father, and spent 20 years in an unloving, unfulfilling marriage. But the past doesn't control her and she doesn't wallow in self-pity. On the contrary! Despite her hardships and difficult upbringing, Cindy has transcended her history and turned her life into a place filled with joy, aliveness and balance.

For Cindy, every day is a new beginning and her lust for life and pursuit of joy, peace and happiness propel her to new heights. She exudes self-confidence and is fearless and unafraid of the road ahead. No matter what the future might present to her, she will overcome the hurdles and reach the finish line with dignity and grace.

Cindy has learned how to "be," how to transcend the negative mind chatter that often defeats others, and how to live life to the fullest.

She is gregarious but claims her privacy when she needs it. She is ambitious and pursues her goals with hard work and focus.

She is non-judgmental and surrounds herself with such a diverse group of people that you would think she had commandeered the United Nations into her circle of friends.

Cindy is genuinely interested in supporting other people's dreams and hopes and she often guides them into making those dreams a reality.

Cindy's desire and willingness to share her journey are intended to make your journey a little bit easier. Her hope is that your answers to the many questions she asked herself during her journey will guide you to the life of joy that she has found! I can't think of a better reason to commit to the journey that awaits you in "Is That All There Is…The Journey Within".

Jeanne Foege

Introduction

I have the ability to communicate with God and clients come to me to hear what God has to say about their lives. After the session they say, "Wow, I feel so much better after speaking with you." They have a sense of relief when they hear what God has to say and how relevant it is to their life. They always want to know how I am able to communicate with God and convey His message to them. They ask, "How do you know this?" I simply say, "I don't, but God does. God knows you and He speaks through me." I let them know they too can do what I do and encourage them to do so.

My ability to communicate with God did not come easily or early in my life. In fact, it did not come at all until I was faced with so much unhappiness that life just didn't seem worth living.

Life's struggles – from an unhappy childhood in an alcoholic family to an unloving marriage and a job that I didn't love – claimed all of my spirit and I found myself neck-deep in the quicksand of life, ready to go under.

I struggled my entire life to be happy and it seems like such an easy goal, doesn't it? But if you are like me, a person who spends a lot of time running around, keeps busy, avoids what you're feeling because you don't like how you feel, forsakes knowing yourself, ignores your heart, remains independent and leans on no one, then maybe you know what I'm talking about. The struggle seems never-ending and the search for happiness unattainable.

The impetus for my true search began with the death of my father. Throughout my childhood years my Dad was never there for me. When I reached adulthood and left home we were estranged. Years later, when I learned of his passing, I went to bed and cried out, "Dad, why couldn't I forgive you?" Suddenly something touched me. Startled, I jumped out of bed and said, "What was that? Who is here?" Then I saw a presence.

I wondered if there could really be life after death? At that moment, when I felt my Dad's presence, I knew the answer was absolutely "yes." There was no need to convince anyone or even myself. I knew what I saw, what I felt. I also knew that I had to understand what had just happened.

At the same time, my entire world was changing, blowing up to be exact. My marriage ended, I disliked myself and my job, I was unhappy, and I was heading to the bottom.

So what happens when you hit bottom? I stayed there for a while. I wasn't eating or sleeping. Completely unhappy with myself and my circumstances, my journey, alas, began. Questions started popping up in my mind, questions that had never occurred to me before. I had never tried to answer why I was so unhappy – I was too busy ignoring me! Immobilized and stuck, I felt a need to seek God and the meaning of my life. God had never been a presence in my life; I was clueless about having a relationship with Him. But somehow, it was God I turned to and it was God who started answering my questions. You will read firsthand what I have learned along the way on my healing journey.

God told me to write this book, saying that it would help many, so I listened to Him and we wrote this book.

By asking yourself the same questions I asked myself, you can travel a similar journey of discovering who you are. You too will find happiness, love, joy and peace on your journey, just as I have. I have road-tested what is contained in this book and it works! I am honored to share my journey of self-discovery with you.

God has a way of giving ordinary people, people like you and me, the ability to do extraordinary things.

Amazing Grace!

Cindy :)

How To Use This Workbook

"Is That All There Is…The Journey Within" is an **inner** workbook journal. It requires time, thought, and introspection. It requires writing answers to questions and looking at issues you may not want to address. It requires honesty, dedication to finding your truth, and really getting to know yourself.

For me my truth is God and knowing who I truly am. We are each on a journey of self-discovery and self-fulfillment in our own way, seeking our own truth for our self.

This workbook is my soulful rise from the depths of despair to a life of happiness, joy, love and peace. On this journey, it is worth sharing my experiences, wisdom and questions so you can travel a journey of self-discovery, self-fulfillment and living your life purpose.

It is not necessary to answer the questions in any particular order. You can go to any chapter in the book that is an area in your life you want to address. Your journey is a lifelong process and requires a commitment, so take whatever time you need for yourself.

During my discovery I learned I was able to hear God; you are too. God gave me this workbook to write. I know this book will help you even if you only answer the questions that are given to you. You do not have to believe in God in order to use this workbook, it will still work!

At the end of each chapter, you will learn about my discoveries, habits and revelations. You too will discover a new you and you will know who you are and how to love yourself. Investing time in yourself is so important, there is only one you and you are indeed a prize!

New Beginnings

Chapter 1

Am I Happy?

What eludes me may find its way to me,
if I only get out of the way and just be.

Chapter One

In This Chapter	➤ Why am I not happy? ➤ Do I consider myself a success? ➤ How can I maintain a state of happiness?

I came home from Target after buying a new sweater, marveling to myself, "Why not?" I chose to indulge myself with some new fall clothes. Suddenly I remembered it was my friend's birthday, so I picked up the phone and asked him how he was celebrating his special day. He replied that he was packing his parents' clothes and other items they had accumulated over the years. What would he do with all their stuff? I thought of the sweater I had just bought and how ironic it was that we accumulate stuff throughout the span of our lives and then, in the end, we get rid of it. I thought, "Is that what it's all about? Is that all there is?"

At that moment I realized in the blink of an eye that I had aged. All these questions started popping into my head: Where had all my years gone? What was it I still wanted to do? My clock was running; it never seemed to stop. As a self-employed single female professing to be spiritual, I was questioning if I would ever be happy. What makes me happy? I had accomplished a lot and I had experienced so many changes during the past ten years - ending a marriage, starting a new romantic relationship, ending my new relationship, moving several times, and transitioning through several careers - that I felt I had come a long way. Each experience added something new to my life. Each experience felt like a birthing process – like I was giving birth to myself over and over again. And sometimes, just like childbirth, it hurt.

I was glad to have come so far, but it seemed like I was always starting all over again.

I remembered watching Oprah. Her guest wrote about a subject that interested me. The show set off a trigger that inspired this book because after watching it

Am I Happy?

> I heard a voice in my head say:
>
> *Go ahead and write this book. It will help you and many others.*

The voice and I began a dialogue. I had questions, lots of questions

> I ask:
>
> *Hmm, help others to do what?*

> I hear:
>
> *To finally be happy!*

> I ask:
>
> *But how does one get there?*

Chapter One

I needed my little voice from within to know that there was nothing more for me to want.

> I hear:
>
> *There is nothing more for you to do except to be happy and enjoy what one may through this mundane existence.*

> I ask:
>
> *How can you use the word "mundane" when you refer to life?*

> I hear:
>
> *It is in the beauty of the routine, the mundane that you can find life's truth. You fail to see the existence of the miracle of each day if you feel your tasks are meaningless and insignificant. Each act, though it may be random, can be met with kindness. The truth is this: you are all you can be by being you, right here, right now. Make every moment count. You count for something always and everywhere you go.*

> I say:
>
> *So just being me is a big thing?*

Am I Happy?

> I hear
>
> *It is a big deal!*

But what do I do with me as this big deal?

When all is said and done am I truly me? Am I living what I believe? Am I doing my best each and every day remembering this deep truth that comes from within: that I am a child of God?

What does being God's child truly mean? I've heard it means that I am loved as I am. But do I know it, feel it and believe it? God does love me! God is my Father so shouldn't my relationship with God and myself count for something? Since God's love is unconditional, do I feel His unconditional love in all areas of my life?

"*Is That All There Is*" kept playing in my head. Have you ever tried to discover the answer to this question? Have your thoughts and feelings haunted you? From the moment you begin your life you try to figure out what it is you want and what you want to do. Some people are so good at figuring it out right out of the gate that they make quick and easy decisions; they seem to have a plan for their entire life.

I have made some impulsive decisions along the way. There were times I should have slowed down when it came to making decisions. Many times I found myself without a clue about what it was I truly wanted. I thought I had a tentative plan. Heck, maybe you think you don't even have a choice. I seemed to love so many things, but what was the thing I loved the most? And what was the point in doing it? As time keeps slipping away I ask myself, "What really makes me happy?" Do I even know? I also wonder if and when I finally figure out what it is I want and actually obtain it, will I then finally be content? So with these thoughts in mind, I wanted to explore what I was feeling. Am I happy?

Being a spiritual woman and supposedly having my act together still did not help to answer the question of what was the "something" that was still lurking inside of me.

Chapter One

What was it I truly wanted to do with the time I had left? Who did I want to spend it with? What, where and when was my next move? Should I even plan it? Struggling most of my life in despair I now desired joy seven days a week in spite of circumstances and situations that arose. I was determined not to lose the sense of joy deep in my soul. I had finally found it and wanted to hold on to it. Was that even possible with God since God was now in my life? Was there such a thing as karma and what was mine? When would I stop feeling emotional pain?

Was it possible to be whisked off and feel as though I was living in the Land of Oz? It seemed that you are here one minute and then the next you cease to exist through death. As you are pulled from the ranks, it is like your tour of duty is up and it is time for you to go. You've disappeared and the ones you left behind go on. Or do they? Some may be forever changed through loss, some have an awakening, and others remain stuck. When I die, I now know heaven will be my home. So, with that in mind, I profess, "Oh, fellow space travelers who are here with me, one by one we will all cease to exist in our current human form." It reminds me of the Honeymooner's expression "To the moon, Alice."

Where do you think you will go when you die? As we get caught up in day-to-day living, sometimes we forget we will not be here forever. "Beam me up, Scottie" is what I stated so many times in the past when I felt I did not want to remain here a minute longer. But my life was not Star Trek. Do you know what I'm talking about? Have you ever felt this way?

What I learned about spiritual matters and life took a while. When I looked around there were people who were no longer in my life. Some had moved, some I outgrew, and others had died. The death of my mother came to mind. She was no longer there to talk to or visit. When my Mom was alive there was some type of comfort in knowing that she worried about me and cared about my life. Sometimes I would share a lot, sometimes not a word. We were never particularly close, but we grew closer as we aged. She seemed to regress with age; as the clock advanced, she turned back into a little girl. She needed help with many of her routine activities that she no longer could do herself. I've often noticed that age has a way to mellow one out. But why do we have to wait until we are older to be mellow? I knew my heavenly Mom was now watching me as a woman trying to run her life the best she knew how, but I missed the physical interaction that we had once shared.

I thought about the following questions:

Am I Happy?

Ask yourself...

1. Does my mother, father, or other significant person in my life consider me a success? Why or why not?

_____
_____
_____
_____
_____

Ask yourself...

2. Do I consider myself a success? Why or why not?

_____
_____
_____
_____
_____

I ask:

What have I accomplished?

Chapter One

> I hear:
>
> *You've come to know me and it's been an amazing journey for you.*

Ok, here is what I now know about the voices I hear (let me explain that I am clairaudient, which means I hear from God). God speaks through me, providing me with great insight. He speaks to you too. **Are you listening?**

So where do I go from here? I admit to God there is supernatural proof that He does exist, to me and to others. I have heard and experienced unbelievable supernatural events so many times. Have you experienced similar events? I know these occurrences are a big deal. While I know these occurrences are a big deal, I realize they are quite normal for all of us if we just recognize them.

> I ask:
>
> *How do I stay excited about life when I'm feeling worn out and tired?*

> I hear God say:
>
> *Focus on what is, rather than on what isn't. The air you breathe is your life force. It's amazing how it flows through you, inside and out, sweeping you clean. With each new breath comes the emergence of a new moment. The journey is simply extraordinary.*

Am I Happy?

I ask:

A moment to do what?

I hear God say:

That is for you to find and figure out. I won't tell you what to do. Joy is a very individual thing.

"Ugh!" I had to think more about joy. What makes people happy? I've got God. I know this: it is a miracle that we eat, breathe and are alive. So before I waste any more time doing something that doesn't float my boat as I play the game of life, I affirm to myself and to God, "Please help me bring in more joy, oodles and oodles of it, so much that my boat tips over. Away I go, merrily, merrily, my life is but a dream."

But I realize my life is not a dream. This is real.

Chapter One

"Is That All There Is?" kept playing through my head.

Chapter 2

That Thing Called *Joy*

*Can it be
that I'm the thing
that will make my heart sing?*

Chapter Two

In This Chapter	➢ What makes you joyful? ➢ How do you feel about yourself? ➢ What do you want out of life?

What is it that makes you joyful? For some it may be going for a drive, getting dirty, not doing housework, sleeping in, not showering, working or not working, the smile of a child, eating a favorite snack, or reading a book. As I pondered that thing called "joy", I realized that this is my journey and no one can walk in my shoes for me. I somehow had to figure out what joy meant to me.

It doesn't seem fair that some people have such an easy walk. I know that if you assemble a group, stack everyone's troubles in a pile, and ask each to pick a trouble, they will likely take back their own. Ok, so I recognize my troubles and say to myself, "What is it that I still want?" Trying to understand life's clues while trying not to be in despair is a trick I had to figure out for myself.

The first thing that popped into my head was to not be so responsible and to take some personal chances. The two areas I chose to make changes in were my marriage and my career. I had spent a huge chunk of time in a marriage and career that did not satisfy me. As I think back, they did not bring me that thing called "joy".

Being a wife was a total disappointment. The man I married was not a good fit. I was lonely, ignored and in self-denial. There was no intimacy. I was stuck – stuck in an unhappy and joyless relationship that took a toll on me personally. Finally after 20 years of marriage, I decided to end it. Luckily, there were no children to worry about. There were financial issues that concerned me, but I was secure in my ability to financially provide for myself. Growing up in an alcoholic household with a Mom who was a child of the Great Depression taught me at a young age how to survive financially.

I was forced to get a job at age 16; it was never an option not to work. In my world it was something you just did. When it came time to choose a career, I decided to become a real estate broker. Since I'm not a morning person, real estate seemed like a very suitable career for me. At least I wouldn't have to get up at 6:00 am, 5 days a week. My real estate career gave me a great deal of insight into the problems other people faced during life's changes- marriage, divorce, death of a spouse, health issues, financial troubles, etc. (you know, the stuff life tosses at us) – and these experiences helped groom me as an intuitive life coach later in life. But this career was not really what I wanted to do.

The major choices I made regarding my marriage and my job did not lead me to finding my spiritual purpose. I had exhausted a ton of time doing the only thing I knew how to do – work. Meanwhile, I had disregarded so many areas of my life, including my own feelings. I was truly ignoring **ME**.

My home environment left me emotionally stunted, as there weren't many hugs or times when we talked about our feelings. Surrounded by anger and constantly being told, "If only I didn't have children" made me feel insignificant and unloved. Where was my mom and dad's joy in being parents? Why did they have me and why did they choose not to be truly close to me? My home experience left me knowing little about myself on an emotional level. I was shut down and I felt a void.

If you had asked me about that thing called "joy" I would have told you that it didn't exist.

I now realize I have other talents and I choose to spend my time doing what I enjoy, which I had not done most of my life. Today how I spend my time working is very important to me. In the past I never allowed myself to make a career change when I didn't enjoy my job. In fact, all of the areas of my life are important to me now. I am finally paying attention to how I feel.

I have learned that if I work all the time, even doing something I love, I will burn out, become cranky or sick and sometimes resentful. I also do not get the chance to spend quiet time with myself or with those I love. When I rest or take a day off, I am refreshed. I also realize that when we play we have an easier time creating something. Relaxation changes and renews our energy so things flow more smoothly.

I have re-evaluated what is important to me and here it is:

1. Continuing to deepen my relationship with God
2. Discovering more about myself
3. Being mindful of my spiritual focus and behavior on a daily basis.
4. Have fun playing
5. Working and enjoying what I do for work

Chapter Two

Ask yourself...

    3. What is important to me?

_____

_____

_____

Ask yourself...

    4. What energizes me?

_____

_____

_____

Sometimes our outlook can change in a moment if we let it.

Ask yourself...

    5. Have I ever changed my outlook? What happened?

_____

_____

_____

When I am stressed, I wonder why I am stressed and why I wasn't following the spiritual knowledge that I learned regarding how to handle life's stress. I promised myself as I wrote this book to pay attention to my own emotional issues, i.e., when I am angry that I don't harbor or run from what I am feeling but rather heal those emotions. I also know God's grace is here to help me. God can heal my emotional stuff.

Learning to write was another surprising twist in the turn of my life, but this was no soap opera. Writing **"Is That All There Is…The Journey Within"** and having been given the gift of discernment made me question, "was this wisdom bringing me joy or confusion?" I knew in the pit of my stomach as I was writing that I was unburying myself from so much of the stuff I had taken on in my life. I realized all of my experiences were taking my life in a whole new direction. But boy did it seem to go slowly. It felt as though it took an entire chunk of my life to learn even the simplest lesson. One of my huge lessons involved **RELATIONSHIPS**. That word turned my world inside out when I began to explore my relationship to God, myself and others.

The steps I had to take to know myself lead me to ask you the following questions:

Ask yourself...

      6. When I look at myself, how do I feel about myself?

_____

_____

_____

_____

Ask yourself...

      7. What do I want in my life?

_____

_____

_____

_____

Chapter Two

Ask yourself...

      8. What is it that I really want to do?

_____
_____
_____
_____

Ask yourself...

      9. What do I have to do to get there?

_____
_____
_____
_____

Ask yourself...

      10. If I achieve these goals, will this bring me joy?

_____
_____
_____
_____

Ask yourself...

    11. What is joy to me?

_____
_____
_____
_____

Often what stirs me to write is the summation of all the things that whirl around inside me. Writing is a way for me to release and to think about what is going on inside of me. My insides may tighten when I want to make changes. If I am not sure about something that is going on in my life, I may be afraid. I ask myself "what should I do"?

I now know that when I go within I am fueled by divine wisdom from God as I ask Him to help me stay peaceful. God knows my next move and He will give me the answers to my many questions if I ask Him. I have reached the half waypoint in my life and time is whizzing by, so it's important to me to have God's help.

So I ask myself if I would be fully satisfied with my life if I were told that it would end tomorrow? Would that kick-start me to feel joy?

What about now?
Am I going to live another moment without joy?
Am I going to live another moment without knowing God? If I do know God am I going to ask Him to help me feel joy?

Ask yourself...

    12. What would I put off and re-prioritize now?

_____
_____
_____
_____

Chapter Two

Ask yourself...

      13. Do I complain and whine all the time? Why or why not?

___
___
___
___

Ask yourself...

      14. If I'm not having any fun, why not?

___
___
___
___

Boy, do I get annoyed with the nitty gritty details of life. They are so time consuming. But understanding and feeling joy is a detail I had to figure out.

I ask:

How do I experience joy in my life?

> I hear God say:
>
> *Live life in the moment, not in the future.*

Okay, so being in the moment would help me appreciate the here and now. I have ignored my writing lately. I always seem to be distracted by something else. Its funny how we let the distractions pull us away from what it is we long for. I would love to be a bestselling author so why wasn't I staying focused on being one? Or wasn't I sure this was what God wanted for my life? Maybe I was actually afraid of my own success!

Ask yourself...

15. Am I afraid of success? Why or why not?

_____

_____

_____

_____

This time I made a vow to myself that my book would be finished. I also vowed to feel the light of joy in each day. I decided to set my timer for fifteen minutes to write, which I would log in my calendar. I would not allow myself to be distracted. So out came my timer and I wrote. I used the timer to claim time and space for me. Wow, did I really have to resort to that trick? I guess so. Not really. I believe writing can be very therapeutic for each one of us. As I open up to you about my thoughts and failures, you too may not feel so alone and honestly admit you feel this way too.

As I wrote it occurred to me how keeping one's focus can be challenging. For me the focus on being in the present moment is essential and the thing I was going to choose for all my moments was to feel oodles of joy!!!!!!! When my joy is sucked out of me life becomes hard. I choose to maintain a feeling of joy. Did I have to work on it or can I

Chapter Two

pack joy away in a suitcase and carry it with me? No I had to work on me. Joy couldn't be packed but it can be contained inside each one of us. We just have to pull it out.

I have heard it said that our lives are like a book with many chapters. What is my next chapter? What is your next chapter? What do I want my life to be like? I've been told that your early chapters can be the opposite of your ending chapters. With God's help and a positive attitude you can write a different chapter for yourself. So as the coauthor of my current chapters I have decided to fill them with lots of happiness. There are many books and writers and if we could each write about what we have learned in our life and compile it into one main book I would title it "<u>The True Way Of Living Life.</u>"

Ask yourself...

      16. Do I choose a joyful path for myself?

_____
_____
_____
_____

I ask:

What about my future?

> I hear God say:
>
> *The future is not important if the present is not appreciated. The future is what is to be, but the present moment is what is. What is this force of life that is in you? It is in you each waking day. It is what fuels you, feeds you, the breath force is what takes you through each moment. Figure out those moments and you'll figure out your life. Notice all that surrounds you? There is simply beauty everywhere. Where is the beauty in you?*

With that profound talk I continued to contemplate. The one thing I knew for sure was that my choices and decisions had to originate from my heart. No more avoidance of that organ! I did that routine for too long. The heart is what stirred me, broke me, opened me up, and melted me. It got me stirring when I left my marriage, when I met a new man, when I lost someone, when I loved someone, and when I hurt someone. Ok, so I was going to feel my heart to help me understand *"is that all there is?"*

> I ask:
>
> *So what's next on the plan?*

> I hear God say:
>
> *Figure out the plan. Analyze your goals. Are they pure? Are they true for you? Take some quiet time for yourself to identify your needs.*

Chapter Two

> I say:
>
> *What are my needs? I want to be loved and valued.*

> I hear God say:
>
> *Go deeper than that.*

I want to radiate pure joy, beam with it, and feel it even in my toes.

As a human being with so much to learn, why can't I always assimilate what I learn and put it to use in my daily life? Knowing that life is not permanent and that my time is temporary I wondered:

Ask yourself...

      17. Am I enjoying each and every second? Why or why not?

_____
_____
_____
_____

Ask yourself...

    18. What type of outlook will I have this week?

_____
_____
_____
_____

Ask yourself...

    19. Why is it I let certain things get to me? What can I do to not take it in?

_____
_____
_____
_____

I ask:

God, why do I feel what I am feeling?

I hear God say:

Keep going deeper.

Chapter Two

> I ask:
>
> *Deeper to where?*

> I hear God say:
>
> *You will know,*
> *You will see the best is yet to come.*

> I say:
>
> *I don't even have a clue how to get to that space.*

> I hear God say:
>
> *Keep writing. You soon will. I won't let you down. This book's a keeper.*

While most of us spend our entire time being busy, it is during the quiet moments that our intuition will speak to us, if we just slow down to listen.

I hear God say:

You see you are getting to that point, the point of understanding. You have found your home in the comfort of knowing me. The time here is a space shuttle ride. The infinite span of time is hard to conjure up, it's hard to fathom. There is nothing to be disturbed about, for nothing lasts forever.

I say:

So what's the point? What is the mission?

I hear God say:

The mission is getting to know you.

I say:

What makes me happy?

The key questions are:

Chapter Two

Ask yourself...

    20.   Do I have "joy" right now in my life?

_____
_____
_____
_____

Ask yourself...

    21.   If I continue my current path and project my journey's completion will I be satisfied?

_____
_____
_____
_____

Ask yourself...

    22.   Do I know God? How can I improve my relationship with Him?

_____
_____
_____
_____

Ask yourself...

    23. Do I want more out of my life? What is my level of contentment?

_____

_____

_____

_____

Ask yourself...

    24. Do I want to move forward? If not, what am I afraid of?

_____

_____

_____

_____

Ask yourself...

    25. Do I like myself? Do I enjoy spending time alone?

_____

_____

_____

_____

Chapter Two

I say:

Do I like the most important person - myself?

I hear God say:

You are getting it.
Do you like yourself?
Do you know who you are?

I say:

I hope God what you are telling me is going to help heal me

I hear God say:

You have no affliction.
You aren't damaged.
You are going on the journey of getting to know yourself.

I say:

But, God, there is affliction. People do suffer and have pain?

I hear God say:

The pain comes when you don't think I care about what is going on in your life. The healing comes when you believe you are loved by me. You can turn your despair into joy

I say:

Is there something I need to take or bring with me on my life's journey?

I hear God say:

Your heart's desire will give you what you want, but it is not about getting what you want. It is about being. It is about peace and contentment.

I ask:

But what if I feel there is something lacking?

I hear God say:

There is nothing missing. Your life is a temporary state, which can be changed

Chapter Two

> I say:
>
> But if I don't have what I want, how can I be happy?

> I hear God say:
>
> *It is simple. It is this - you have you. No one can take you away from you. You will always be your best company. Appreciate who you are.*

Ask yourself...

    26. When I am alone, what do I enjoy doing with my time?

_____
_____
_____
_____

Ask yourself...

    27. When I am with others, what do I enjoy doing?

_____
_____
_____
_____

Since I am always so busy, the first thing that came to mind was taking the time to do nothing. Can doing nothing really be fun? You bet it can! I've often said that and people sarcastically say, "Right, Cindy." But truthfully, time spent reflecting with nowhere to go can be quite exhilarating. There is no checking my watch, no rushing, and no pressure. I can even stop to hear the wind howl, feel the sunshine or drops of rain upon my face, smell the aromatic sea breezes, gleefully watch the snowflakes glisten as they fall, and listen to the symphony of birds. I can watch the flow of life all around me. I am witnessing life all the time, but do I sense and capture the beauty seven days a week?

Ask yourself...

    28. What activities do I consider fun?

_____

_____

_____

Ask yourself...

    29. What things, little or big, bring me joy?

_____

_____

_____

_____

Chapter Two

I'm slowly understanding that there is nothing to get but to just "be."

Do I realize I don't need things to be happy?

> I say:
>
> *But my job keeps me busy all the time and I don't have a chance to have fun.*

> I hear God say:
>
> *I am here.*
> *Life is not a job, but a journey*

> I say:
>
> *Now that is deep!*

> I hear God say:
>
> *The deeper you go, the more you find yourself, and the more you find joy.*

Smile

Chapter Two

Habits   *The Old Cindy*

I didn't appreciate who I was and I didn't know myself. I didn't bother to spend any time getting to know myself or God. I didn't realize how important it was to know and understand myself or that I was a vital part of my life's equation.

Discoveries

I was joyless, I would work all the time and did not take time off to play. I had no clue how to have fun. If you had asked me what I liked to do for fun, I would have said, "I don't know".

Spiritual Revelation

I didn't have a clue who God was. My father was never there for me and since I didn't have a good relationship with my Dad, I could not relate to God as my Father either. A God / Father relationship was foreign and strange to me. My logic was that I couldn't have a relationship with God for he was just like my Dad, and therefore wouldn't be there or care for me either.

Habits

The New Cindy

I now understand what I want and do not want in my life. I choose to have a relationship with myself and with God. I choose to explore life and discover more about myself each and every day.

Discoveries

I discovered "fun" and "fun" is now a daily part of my life. Each week I make sure to schedule something fun to do. I power walk every day. I like to walk on my own so I can go when I want. As I walk I like to pray and reflect. I never miss my walk for it always makes me feel better and it is important to me. I regularly send emails to my friends inviting them to go to the movies. We go to a local movie theater where the admission is only $2.00. I love bargains so I go and see all types of movies.

I go dancing and take dance lessons with my friends. If they can't make it I will go alone; I don't let their schedules stop me from having fun. I find something to be joyful about each day.

Spiritual Revelation

I now realize that God listens to me and cares about every area of my life. If I am not happy it is within my power to find out what is causing me to feel this way. I know it is important to spend time talking and listening to God about the things I hold in my heart and to find out what we can do together to solve any issues I have.

Chapter Two

After reading Cindy's transformation from the "Old Cindy" to the "New Cindy", please turn to chapter 13 and complete your evaluation of the "Old You". Allow at least 21 days after finishing the workbook, and then complete the "New You" section.

Remember change is a process. Like many things in life, *progress takes time.*

»»»» **Take Action** ««««

Choose at least one action you can take now.

➢ Do a fun activity that makes you happy each day this week
➢ Complete a re-prioritized activity today
➢ Don't look at a clock the entire day - let your Spirit direct you.

Chapter 3

What Needs to Change?

What step must I take
to get things done?
Can it all be so simple
aligning with the Holy one?

Chapter Three

In This Chapter	➤ Do you see beauty all around you? ➤ Are you practicing healthy eating, drinking, and exercise habits? ➤ Are your spoken words positive and uplifting or negative and attacking?

So if I am here and God you are with me, then together we are in that great "I Am" presence, the great "I Am" being God, then God is with us every day. Right? We are a team. Wow! This is amazing, but do I believe it? Does this fill me spiritually or are these just words?

I remember times when I would overeat or under eat, depending on my mood. If I was depressed, I would either binge or not eat a thing. If I was bored, eating was something to do. My spiritual hunger tied into my eating habits. Thankfully I now know how to fuel myself on all levels. I think of myself as a car that needs gas. So what am I fueling myself with? I say yes to holistic healthy eating, but I do savor some junk food here and there. The point is not to feel deprived. If I do not take care of myself how will I run? The choice is mine. As I focus on my eating habits, do they tie into "Is That All There Is…The Journey Within"? I know about eating healthy, exercising, staying in shape, and limiting my alcohol intake. When I do those things I feel much better. I do not need alcohol or drugs to alter my state and interfere with my clarity. So what is the purpose of alcohol? It seems to be something we need in our lives and is a part of our social scene.

What Needs to Change?

I ask:

Why do some people drink alcohol excessively?

I hear God say:

To escape pain.

I ask:

But how does it help when it is only temporary?

I hear God say:

A good question. It may temporarily numb the pain or bring joy but it is not a natural state of living, especially in excess. It's a chemical alteration that has wrecked many lives. Can you do without it? Do not let it take hold of you. You can experience joy without it.

Coming from an alcoholic background doesn't mean I disapprove of alcohol. I just know I feel different when I drink. I remember the experiences of feeling hung over or doing something embarrassing and not remembering what I did. I did not like the way this felt or the way I behaved. So if I am working on uncovering myself, how will drinking help? I know it won't.

Chapter Three

When it comes to eating, I love fresh food and foods in their natural state. This is why I love to have a vegetable garden. The garden size doesn't matter; it may be big or small or exist in flowerpots. The importance of gardening is that you have control over your food source.

Vegetable gardens bring the following rewards:
- Witnessing how things grow
- Digging in the dirt
- It's therapeutic
- Organic veggies are healthy for you
- Picking and eating them in their freshest state is healthier and tastier than eating store bought
- Brings you back to the earth
- You become a shepherd who cares for the earth
- You see what is in the environment
- You notice nature as you work with nature
- You appreciate the beauty of landscape

The thought of gardening may not appeal to you, but:
Ask yourself...

30. Can I see the beauty in a garden? What do I see?

_____
_____
_____
_____

What Needs to Change?

Ask yourself...

    31.   Do I see beauty all around?

___

Ask yourself...

    32.   Describe what is beautiful about me?

Chapter Three

The white birch trees are so pure and the roots run so deep. I can relate to the birch trees.
I hear myself say:

"I am to be so pure, pure of white light and truth.
Energy flows thru me; my roots are so deep that nothing shakes me
from feeling and knowing God."

Gardens require water. We too are made of water and we should drink a lot of it.
- ❑ Water detoxifies us
- ❑ It makes our skin glow
- ❑ It hydrates our cells.

Here is a formula for calculating how much water you need to drink on a daily basis:
1. Weigh yourself and note your weight.
2. Take the number of pounds you weigh and multiply that by 2/3.
   That is the number of ounces you should drink every day.
    For example, if you weigh 150 pounds, two thirds of that is 100 and that is how many ounces you should drink daily.
3. Measure out your amount into a container so you can visually see how much water that really is. For example, a can of soda is 12 ounces. That equates to 8 cans of water per day.

Being near water calms me. When I go to the ocean I feel as though I've entered God's living room. As I look out over the ocean, it appears endless. As I walk the beach I smile as I breathe in the salt air. I fantasize about living near the ocean with an ocean view one day, but for now I keep that view in my mind's eye. Where is my waterfront property? Do I really care if I get it? It seems so important, but is it? Can't I go to the ocean when I choose? I know of people who live on the ocean or a lake and never take the time to enjoy it. Does any of this make sense?

Thinking about the ocean reminds me of wearing a bathing suit. With less clothes to camouflage me I think of exercise and how I need to keep my body in shape. My favorite form of exercise is walking, during which inspiring thoughts come to me. Walking and breathing the outside air helps me hear the voice of God. My walks have a way of grounding me to the earth as stress releases from my body. After a walk I always feel better. So if that is the case, why do I fight them? Why do we fight exercise if it makes us feel better?

Why do I love to walk?
- ❑ My energy moves.
- ❑ I shift into a relaxed state.
- ❑ When I am stressed, walking melts away the tensions of the day.
- ❑ My muscles release and stretch.
- ❑ I focus on my breathing.
- ❑ I value my body.

Chapter Three

- ☐ I recharge.
- ☐ I refuel.
- ☐ I detoxify as I am circulating my energy.
- ☐ I take time out for me.
- ☐ Since I walk outside, I see nature.
- ☐ Even indoor walking is good.
- ☐ Walking is about movement.
- ☐ I pray when I walk, knowing each step I take is with God.

Ask yourself...

33. What exercise do I like? How often do I exercise? PS...(Did you today?)

_____
_____
_____
_____

We talked a little about eating and exercising, but do we consider the weight of our words?

WEIGHT OF MY WORDS

Ask yourself…

34. What tone of voice do I use to speak to others?

_____
_____
_____
_____

What Needs to Change?

Ask yourself...

35. Am I expressing myself with optimism or anger? Give an example:

___

Ask yourself...

36. Do my words come from love and joy or doubt and fear? Why?

___

Ask yourself...

37. Am I able to express personal concerns or does it make me feel uncomfortable? Why or why not?

___

Chapter Three

Ask yourself…

38. Do I intend to say something positive but it is interpreted as negative? How can I change that?

_____
_____
_____
_____

Ask yourself...

39. When I have personal dialogue, do I put my foot in my mouth? What can I do to be more graceful?

_____
_____
_____
_____

Ask yourself…

40. Do I pray to God to help me say what I should say before I say it?

_____
_____
_____
_____

Ask yourself...

    41.   When I speak, do I speak from my heart? Why or why not?

_____

_____

_____

Ask yourself…

    42.   Do my words and actions capture people's hearts or push them away? Why do I do this?

_____

_____

_____

_____

Ask yourself...

    43.   Do I feel there is something I still need to say? And to whom?

_____

_____

_____

_____

Chapter Three

Ask yourself...

    44.   Am I getting closer to **"Is That All There Is"**?

_____
_____
_____
_____

Be open to change

Chapter Three

Habits   *The Old Cindy*

I didn't exercise or worry about what I ate. I could consume a bag of chips in a night, eat candy every night before bed and drink lots of soda during the day.

Discoveries

I didn't take enough personal time for myself. Life always had a way of getting in the way and when it did, I would let it. If I was invited to a special event at a time when I had to work, I would always choose the work. And since I was really busy I didn't feel I had time to exercise. I never paid attention to what I ate and the effect it might be having on my health. I would run around aimlessly working all the time, I wasn't happy.

Spiritual Revelation

I never paid attention to or realized the power of the spoken word. I didn't think it was important how I said something. I would mask and cover so many of my innermost feelings. No one ever knew what I was truly thinking or feeling. I was a master at hiding my emotions, much to my detriment!

Habits

I walk almost every day to release stress, move energy, detox and stay in shape. It is a gift I give myself every day. I rarely have soda, I enjoy junk food on occasion and I've cut way back on sugar. In addition, I now drink plenty of water throughout the day.

If I explode at someone, I pull myself back and question what it was that caused me to behave in that manner. I am aware of how I am behaving and figure out what I need to do to stop inappropriate behavior. I also pray and ask God to calm me down or let me see what I am being shown through my behavior.

Discoveries

I pay attention to what I do, how I spend my time and what I choose to eat. Being mindful of these key areas in my life has turned out to be such a good thing for me, resulting in feeling and looking healthier. I now have a healthy outlook on life. I value my time and myself. I continually reflect upon the key areas in my life and how I feel.

Spiritual Revelation

I learned about the power of the spoken word and how my words set things in motion. I help to create things in my life by what I speak about. What I focus on often has a way of happening, so I pay attention to what I am thinking about and why.

I also know God wants me to share with Him and others what it is I am feeling. Rather than reacting to my feelings by ranting and raving, I talk about and share them. I am not meant to stuff everything away inside of me without letting it out in a proper fashion. I choose not to attack but to act with love.

Chapter Three

After reading Cindy's transformation from the "Old Cindy" to the "New Cindy", please turn to chapter 13 and complete your evaluation of the "Old You". Allow at least 21 days after finishing the workbook, and then complete the "New You" section.

Remember *change is a process.* Like many things in life, *progress takes time.*

»»»»» Take Action «««««

Choose at least one action you can take now.

- ➢ Exercise for 10 minutes each day.
- ➢ Say something kind or inspirational to someone. It only takes one person to make an effect that ripples to many others.
- ➢ Eat nutritional meals this week.

Chapter 4

My Aspirations

I wish I was
I wish I might
Believe in all my dreams
This very night.

Chapter Four

In This Chapter	➤ What are your hopes and dreams? ➤ Who are your role models? ➤ What qualities do you admire in others? ➤ Have you ever witnessed a miracle?

Do the hopes and dreams that we cherish represent what we want in the first place? You have heard the expression "be careful what you pray for, you just may get it". When I think about my life I need to go within to figure out what it is I want to have in my life and why.

HOPES AND DREAMS
Ask yourself…

    45.   What do I hope for and dream about?

___
___
___
___

Ask yourself…

    46.   Am I moving in my desired direction – what is it? What obstacles are in the way?

___
___
___

My Aspirations

_____
_____

Ask yourself…

    47.   What areas of my life seem incomplete?

_____
_____
_____
_____

Ask yourself…

    48.   What areas do I need to work on or change?

_____
_____
_____
_____

Aspirations are necessary to achieve happiness.

Ask yourself…

    49.   Who am I aspiring to become?

_____
_____
_____
_____
_____

Ask yourself…

50. What do I want to be known for and by whom?

_____
_____
_____
_____

Ask yourself…

51. If my dreams do not come true, will I feel that I have failed?

_____
_____
_____
_____

Ask yourself…

52. Will I feel good about myself either way?

_____
_____
_____
_____
_____
_____

My Aspirations

Do you realize that if you don't accomplish your dreams you are complete just as you are. Aspirations are wonderful if they are for the right reasons; but you need to ask yourself the following…

LIFE PURPOSE

What is God's purpose for your life? Often you may think your career ties into your purpose and what you are supposed to be doing. Part of your purpose may tie into what you do for work but it also ties into just being. Life is not just about doing! As you evaluate your career path and your life's work, you will want to focus on what fuels you rather than depletes you. Many of us don't have a clue what it is we love or how to get paid for the work we would love to do. So let us begin by evaluating what you do for work.

Ask yourself…

    53.   What is the first thing that pops into my mind that I am good at?

_____
_____
_____
_____

Ask yourself...

    54.   What job did I enjoy most of all? Why?

_____
_____
_____
_____

Chapter Four

Ask yourself...

    55.   What was the job I liked least of all? Why?

_____

_____

_____

_____

Ask yourself...

    56.   Based on my likes and dislikes from above, what career path may be best for me?

_____

_____

_____

_____

When we strive towards goals that we feel guided and led to, does it make any sense in the grand scheme of things when they don't turn out the way we expect them to? Oh, did I mention my plan is this: to have the **best** life I can have. Do we know that we have an abundant God who is our Father who loves us? Don't parents want the best for their kids? Do you feel that God will help you fulfill the plan He has for you in your life? Do you ask Him to help you do just that?

My Aspirations

ROLE MODELS IN YOUR LIFE

Ask yourself...

    57.   If I were going to be taught more about life, who would my teacher be?

_____

_____

_____

_____

I have the number one teacher, so do you and the perfect opportunity to continue to ask my teacher (God) more questions.

Ask yourself...

    58.   Name four people you consider your teachers who have helped you in your life. What did they teach you?

_____

_____

_____

_____

Ask yourself...

    59.   Name four of your friends. What do you value in them?

_____

_____

_____

_____

Chapter Four

Ask yourself…

60. Name four people who make you feel appreciated and special. How do they make you feel special?

_____
_____
_____

Ask yourself…

61. Name four people you enjoy spending time with. What makes spending time with them enjoyable?

_____
_____
_____
_____

Ask yourself...

62. What do these people who know me the best think I am good at and why?

_____
_____
_____
_____

My Aspirations

Ask yourself...

63. If I don't allow anyone to truly know me, why not?

_____
_____
_____
_____

Ask yourself...

64. If I can't answer any of these questions, do I feel all alone or am I content?

_____
_____
_____
_____

Now let's switch gears.

Chapter Four

ACCOMPLISHMENTS

Ask yourself...

      65.   Am I a self-motivated, goal-oriented person or do I lack motivation? Am I ok with it?

___
___
___
___

Ask yourself...

      66.   Do I allocate sufficient time for my personal life?

___
___
___
___

Ask yourself...

      67.   Am I caught up in what feels like a rat race? Or is my pace of life fine?

___
___
___
___

Ask yourself...

    68.   If this were my last day on earth, with whom would I spend it?

_____

_____

_____

_____

I am aspiring to be so many things. Too many aspirations can leave me feeling depleted, as though I need to do everything to prove something. When will my "to do" list end?

Am I recharged by what I do? If not, I wind up becoming exhausted with room only for rest. When I choose to rest I realize that it is for the best, for I know enough to take care of me.

Am I not the most valuable possession? In an airplane we are given instructions to put our oxygen masks on first before we help someone else. We need to take care of ourselves before we can assist someone else.

Ask yourself...

    69.   Am I taking care of myself? How? What do I do to ensure that?

_____

_____

_____

_____

Chapter Four

Ask yourself...

    70.   Is my current lifestyle fueling or emptying my engine? What is causing either feeling?

_____

_____

_____

_____

Ask yourself...

    71.   Are my accomplishments in harmony with my Spirit?

_____

_____

_____

_____

Ask yourself...

    72.   Do I know I am of value? What do I value about myself?

_____

_____

_____

_____

My Aspirations

Ask yourself...

73. Do I aspire to know myself? How do I do that?

_____
_____
_____
_____

Ask yourself...

74. As I am working my way through this book, do I aspire to know God better?

_____
_____
_____
_____

Ask yourself...

75. Am I open to experiencing the endless miracles in each day? Can I name a miracle in my life today?

_____
_____
_____
_____

Chapter Four

Ask yourself...

76. Have I lost every ounce of myself, forgotten what I am about and simply given up my dreams?

___
___
___

I ask God:

What do you have to say about this teaching?

I hear God say:

It's a powerful one. Stop preaching. They'll get it one way or another, as will you. You've asked and asked. The heavens hear your cries; it's your call. Take the long way or the highway; the road always leads home.

I ask God:

Is there something I should add to or take out of this book?

I hear God say:

Not a thing. It is perfectly written. Keep on going, but in the silence, feel the presence, the Holy presence. Learn to feel me in all the moments of your life.

My Aspirations

Dream

Chapter Four

Habits   *The Old Cindy*

I worked and didn't care if I liked it. I didn't hope or dream about anything. I never wanted to go out, and making changes of any type never seemed an option. I believed you were stuck in your path and that it was simply the way it was.

Discoveries

I didn't know I had a purpose in my life, I never really thought about it; it wasn't important to me. Work was work! It didn't matter if I enjoyed it; it was something you were supposed to do to pay your bills. I didn't have the luxury of staying home and keeping house. I used to be married and my husband, at the start of our marriage, told me I had to go to work and get a job. It wasn't an option. I thought I was supposed to stay home and take care of the house and him. Work was something you always did. I didn't know you could take time off or take a leave of absence. The only way I did that was when I was sick.

I didn't appreciate who I was or what my gifts were. I had no idea what I truly liked to do for work. I also thought you had to work hard all the time to earn a living.

Spiritual Revelation

I relied on me to support myself and I felt as though I didn't have any help. I always felt on my own and could not depend upon anyone. What I learned as a child carried over into my marriage. I was extremely independent; I didn't know how to ask for help.

My Aspirations

Habits   *The New Cindy*

I now do what I love when it comes to work. I pray, visualize and think about what I would like to have happen in my life. I now have hopes and dreams. I dream about what I want to experience in my life and fantasize about it happening, all along smiling inside. I am also fine if it doesn't happen because I know how to have fun playing out the scenario in my Spirit and mind. I pay attention to what I think about and focus my thoughts on being positive.

Discoveries

I understand we all have a purpose and plan for our life. Many of the things that happened to us in our past were part of God's plan for where He is leading us in our life. I know I am here as a teacher to help others with their inner struggles and beliefs. I care that the work I am doing is part of God's plan for my life. It is important to me not just to work but to love what I do for work. I don't worry about paying my bills for I know the money will be there since I am following my passion. I also know we serve a generous God.

Spiritual Revelation

I am not alone. I have helpers - God, Jesus, friends and family help and watch out for me. I am able to talk with God any time and ask Him what I need in my life. I pray and thank God for helping me meet all of my needs every day.

I will ask people in my life to help me. Friends of mine are helping put together this book; I am blessed by each one of them. I appreciate their time and help and I am so grateful for having them in my life. I feel that appreciation is a spiritual principal where you realize you are worthy and deserving of many good things. I also understand it is important to balance my energy and give something back in return.

Chapter Four

After reading Cindy's transformation from the "Old Cindy" to the "New Cindy", please turn to chapter 13 and complete your evaluation of the "Old You". Allow at least 21 days after finishing the workbook, and then complete the "New You" section.

Remember *change is a process.* Like many things in life, *progress takes time.*

»»»»» Take Action «««««
Choose at least one action you can take now.

➤ State out loud one of your dreams while you dance to the thought of your dream coming true.
➤ Meditate and reflect for 15 minutes twice this week.
➤ In the next 24 hours, accomplish one action leading you closer to a goal.
➤ Ask a role model teacher to help you with your goal. Let them be someone with whom you are able to check in on your progress.
➤ Make a bucket list!

Chapter 5
The Drama - Is it Holding Me Back?

*The curtain comes down, the act ends,
did the plot turn out the way I thought it would?
Did I give all I could?*

Chapter Five

In This Chapter	➢ Why the drama? ➢ Are you writing your script as a tragedy or a comedy? ➢ What role are you choosing to enact – lead, villain, victim, or hero? ➢ Do you follow through on your promises? ➢ Do you accomplish goals you have set? ➢ How do you wish to be remembered?

Your life is like a play.

I ask:

But why the drama?

I hear God say:

It's how you learn.
Choose another play.
Some learn quickly while others falter and go through it all over again.
Be patient, be kind, and be tolerant.

The Drama - Is It Holding Me Back?

> I say:
>
> *Wow, I get to choose another play? Then I choose a love story with humor.*

There are so many choices and decisions I would have changed. I reflect upon them as time allows, but I realize now it was as it should have been. They helped shape me into who I am. How I feel is crucial. If I never reflect, how will I truly know the deeper meaning of anything?

> I ask God:
>
> *How should I view time?*

> I hear God say:
>
> *Time is not your enemy but your friend, befriend it, it doesn't haunt you. It is mysterious to you, but there is no mystery in the mystery. Arise and feel the light of day. You can choose to keep things mysterious or you can choose to learn and grow. Either way it is your call, ask and it will be found.*

I am learning that I am important.
- ❏ I am the lead character.
- ❏ I will choose my role.
- ❏ I will choose what I believe in.
- ❏ I will choose what I feel.
- ❏ I will either like the role I have picked or I will choose to play another role.

Chapter Five

Circle your answer...

What role am I playing?
Widower
Widow
Single
Separated
Divorced
Married

Circle your answer...

What part do I want to play next?
A couple
A dad
A mom
Single
Married
Being part of a family

Circle your answer...

Does my character choose to be...
Happy
Sad
Independent
Dependent
Peaceful
Anxious
Balanced
Off-centered
Content
Discontent
One who speaks my truth
One who keeps everything inside
Proud
Ashamed
Open minded
Judgmental
Warm hearted
Cold shoulder
Honest
A liar

Chapter Five

Ask yourself...

When it comes to my role in my life:
Am I in good physical shape?_____
_____
Do I keep a check on myself?_____
_____
Do I follow through with what I promise to do for others?_____
_____
Do I follow through with my goals?_____
_____
Do I walk the talk?_____
_____

Circle your answer...

When the curtains close, how do I want my character to be remembered?
I lived a life all alone
I left behind a legacy
I made a difference
I was an active participant in life
I was educated
I became a world traveler
I was Spiritual
I was a humanitarian
I was rich
I made many friends
I was content
I was happy
I knew God

I was loved and will be missed
I took care of those I loved
Hearts were touched knowing me
I was a good parent

And finally...have I asked the Director, I mean God, what He thinks of my performance? I am the lead role in my play called "Life".

Ask God...

     77. It is your turn to ask God, what he thinks of your performance.

_____

_____

_____

_____

Ask yourself...

     78. Is my role consistent with what I imagined my life would be?

_____

_____

_____

_____

If the answer is yes, hurray! You are happy with your life. This is great! But if the answer is no...

Chapter Five

Ask yourself...

79. If I am miserable or anxious, how and what do I need to change?

_____
_____
_____
_____
_____

Ask yourself...

80. What aspects of my life can God help me with?

_____
_____
_____
_____

It is up to <u>YOU</u> to take the time to focus on believing something totally different for yourself. When I examine my thoughts and seek answers to questions and feelings that disturb me, I can then work on what needs to change inside of me. When I change my viewpoint my life looks different. I have done it and so can you! We are not so different. We have much in common.

It doesn't take a rocket scientist to realize that you fuel yourself with your attitudes, thoughts and beliefs.

I now understand what is and what isn't important. I consider this a gift. The most important thing to me is me. For after the children, husband or wife, those who come and go, the promotion or demotion, and the many endless changes we experience, I still have me and you still have you. I will hang on to myself. I will never let myself go. I am my own project. Aim high, aim low. It is your call, but aim.

The Drama - Is It Holding Me Back?

I ask God:

Anything else I need to share?

I hear God say:

The aim is not complete if you think the universe is void of any control. The universe is at the controls to guide and assist you. Never be afraid to ask what it is you truly want.

I ask God:

Ok, what about the people I encounter?

I hear God say:

Let's discuss that next.

On with the drama, I mean on with the show. Remember you choose your character. Play your part well.

Chapter Five

Habits

The Old Cindy

I didn't pay attention to the role I was playing in my life. I did not feel successful in my real estate career even though I was good at it. Since I felt that I could lose my clients if they weren't my priority all the time, I worked around the clock and missed out on other areas of life.

Discoveries

I played the role of the girl who looked like she had it all, but didn't. I had the big house, a Mercedes and a husband, but I was lonely, and unhappy. I felt like a walking zombie completely dead inside. I pretended to be happy but wasn't. I sometimes looked at happy people and wondered what they did that made them so happy. I just didn't get it.

Spiritual Revelation

I would rush around all the time never taking time to smell the roses. I didn't even look at roses yet alone think about them. Yes, I would like to have roses sent to me, what girl wouldn't, but I sure did not notice them in the great outdoors! I didn't even understand that I was one of God's roses.

Everything was labor intensive. Things had to look perfect. I didn't know how to relax how to meditate or how to spend time reflecting on my life.

Habits

The New Cindy

I know the role I choose to play in my life now. I choose to balance my work and my personal life. I am a priority for the first time and I know what I want and am not afraid to ask for it. I understand I am able to make choices. I schedule fun activities throughout the week like going to the movies, inviting friends over, reading great books, making new friends and dining out. These are a few of the things that I like to do.

Discoveries

I love myself and am truly happy. While spending time doing my inner work I learned about myself and it resulted in me liking who I am. I don't feel lonely and I appreciate being alive. I now GET IT! I now am one of those people who others look at and may wonder "why is she so happy"! It's so wonderful to be on the other side of that equation! AMEN!

Spiritual Revelation

I meditate, pray, and slow myself down to listen to God speak to me. I love the quiet time when I am still and I sense what it is I need to know spiritually about my life. It is so relaxing and refreshing, like taking a mini nap.

Chapter Five

After reading Cindy's transformation from the "Old Cindy" to the "New Cindy", please turn to chapter 13 and complete your evaluation of the "Old You". Allow at least 21 days after finishing the workbook, and then complete the "New You" section.

Remember *change is a process.* Like many things in life, *progress takes time.*

»»»» Take Action ««««
Choose at least one action you can take now.

- ➤ Rewrite your script by having your character take action in a new direction.
- ➤ Write down 3 goals to be accomplished in the next week.
- ➤ Accomplish one of your goals today.
- ➤ Follow through with a promise you made.

Chapter 6
The People In Your Life: Love, Loss, and Forgiveness

*The most important person is you,
for you are a masterpiece!*

Chapter Six

In This Chapter	➢ Who are the positive and negative co-actors in your drama? ➢ Do you value yourself and others? ➢ Are your encounters sacred or antagonistic? ➢ Do you love unconditionally and forgive others?

People are important to me. Life should not only be about the material stuff, which can be replaced or thrown away, it should be about people who are invaluable. To me they are catalysts in our lives helping to shape us into whom we are. They can challenge us, teach us, push our buttons, bring us to tears, and make us smile.

I know we are deeply affected by our relationships with our parents, siblings, family members, friends, coworkers, boyfriends, girlfriends, spouses, group associations and employers, and each of these relationships has an impact – positive or negative – on who we are and how we see things.

My relationship with my Dad had an extremely bad effect on me. He was an alcoholic who never showed love or affection. My childhood was not a happy one and I left home as soon as possible after high school. My Dad and I never talked at all after that. He died and we never even said goodbye. Not having a Dad to care for me left a huge void in my life and my relationships have been affected by this experience.

My relationship with my husband of 20 years was lonely and empty and though not abusive, it too was devoid of love and intimacy. Love was foreign to me and when I finally met a man where there was a mutual attraction, which we acted on, he showed me a glimpse of what love could be. The relationship, however, was superficial and didn't last and it catapulted me into reevaluating the relationship I wanted to have with a man.

Even though my relationships fell apart I felt that there was a romantic partner for me out there somewhere and I was determined to find him. When I finally met a man who showered me with love and affection, pampering, and fussing over me, I wasn't used to all the attention. My relationship with him made me realize that there could be so much more to a loving and caring relationship than I had ever imagined was possible

I had close friendships that ended and unfortunately were hurtful. I forever hold their teachings with me for I know that all relationships serve a purpose in my life. Who knows, we may even get back together one day. I am open to it but won't force it to happen. I accept people coming and going. I know it is part of my growth and I need to pay attention to how I grow - that is where I need to focus my thoughts. I can only change myself. I don't stay mad at anyone any longer. I know to forgive them and myself, to talk to them about what may have been hurtful to me or them, and then to move forward.

So let's take a good look at your relationships, what they have meant to you and the effect they have had on you.

RELATIONSHIPS

Ask yourself...

How have these people affected my life in a positive or negative way?

Mom _____

Dad _____

Siblings _____

Grandparents _____

Aunts/Uncles _____

Strangers _____

Cousins _____

Chapter Six

Spouses / partner / significant other _____

Friends _____

Teachers _____

Coworkers _____

Employers _____

Ask yourself...

      81. Who had the most positive influence on me in my life? Why?

_____
_____
_____
_____

Ask yourself...

      82. Who had the most negative influence on me in my life? Why?

_____
_____
_____

Ask yourself...

83. How have these influences affected my current relationships?

_____
_____
_____
_____

Ask yourself...

84. How have I influenced or affected other people?

Positively:
_____
_____
_____
_____

Negatively:
_____
_____
_____
_____

Chapter Six

Ask yourself...

    85. What do I do to develop my relationships?

___

Ask yourself...

    86. What do people do to bring out the best in me?

___

Ask yourself...

    87. What do I do to bring out the best in them?

___

Ask yourself...

88. What characteristics do I admire the most in others?

___

Ask yourself...

89. What characteristics do I dislike the most in people?

___

Ask yourself...

90. Why do I allow people to affect me negatively? How do I react to negative behavior/people?

Chapter Six

Ask yourself...

    91. How do I express my feelings in relationships?

_____
_____
_____
_____

Ask yourself...

    92. In what ways do I show my love and affection?

_____
_____
_____
_____

Ask yourself...

    93. What stops me from expressing how I feel?

_____
_____
_____
_____

Ask yourself...

94. Give examples of people who push your buttons and trigger negative emotions - i.e. anger, envy, etc. Why do you think you react the way you do?

___

Ask yourself...

95. When I get angry with someone, do I resolve my anger or resentment in a positive or negative way?

Chapter Six

Do I feel and know the following:
- I value myself.
- I value others.
- I value the time we spend together.
- I thank others for what they have taught me.
- I feel blessed we have crossed paths with one another.
- Relationships are part of the sacred plan.
- I am here to know God.
- I am here to know myself.
- I am here to heal.
- I am here to love.
- I am here to develop relationships with people.

> I hear God say:
>
> *People are my purpose and passion. My love for each one of you is endless as are the paths of your soul. It is your soul's responsibility to come to know God. I am forever your friend and we will meet again in the end.*

LOVE

My view on relationships is directly affected by my concept of love. The way you view love is essential in your relationships so let's address the way you view love in a relationship.

Ask yourself...

    96. When I love someone, what conditions do I place on our relationship?

_____
_____
_____
_____

Ask yourself...

    97. What are my reasons for placing conditions on our relationship?

_____
_____
_____
_____

Ask yourself...

    98. What does it mean to me to love someone unconditionally?

_____
_____
_____
_____

Chapter Six

Ask yourself...

99. How does God love me unconditionally?

_____
_____
_____
_____

Ask yourself...

100. In what ways do I feel God's unconditional love?

_____
_____
_____
_____

Unconditional love did not feel natural to me and I did not know how to receive it or give it back. I needed to learn more about it so I prayed to understand unconditional love and, boy, was it shown to me. Over the years, God has taught me about unconditional love with so many situations involving the people in my life. There are people who really shouldn't still be in my life, but I chose to forgive them even though they hurt me badly. That is unconditional love. Being able to forgive myself and others is a gift.

As we learn about love, do we become more vulnerable? Yes! I would rather open my heart and be vulnerable than never know or experience love. Wouldn't you too?

Can you still love someone even when you have to say goodbye? Yes, you can. You can always choose to carry people in your heart. So I love God, myself, and my neighbor as best I can. Does that mean everything will be hunky-dory? I think not. But do I know the depth that love will go for me? It may seem that we all come in to this world alone and we return home alone, but we are not really alone, for we are with God and surrounded by His angels at all times.

When we go through challenges, there may be others who are there to help if we let them. When I had challenging times I used to think it would be great if someone would step inside of me and take my place. However, I know that when I go through something difficult it changes me. Life's experiences should help us grow spiritually, gain emotional strength, and open our hearts. It is unfortunate that many people have had personal experiences that push them away from God. I have found that the very things that have brought me to my knees and made me cry have forced me to go within myself. That resulted in bringing me closer to myself and to God. You may say "How can that be?"

LOSS

I ask God:

God, why do you work that way? Why do we have to experience seemingly insurmountable challenges throughout our lives like the loss of a loved one?

I hear God say:

The maturity of the soul knows this: I am as disappointed as you with loss but you need to know it is only temporary. Love is the only permanent thing, it determines who you are. Love is pure. Love is kind, love lacks selfishness, it doesn't like division, and it matures with time. You have reached a maturity that many long for: it's simply this - <u>love yourself</u>.

Chapter Six

I ask God:

How do I handle loss?

I hear God say:

You find yourself and you find others who are exactly where you are at this point in time.

You go to the core of you.

I ask God:

God what do you mean by the core of me?

I hear God say:

It is the part deep inside of you where you store your emotions, your feelings of disappointment and your thoughts of how things should be. You need to allow me to heal and take away what is deep inside of you as you heal and grow from it all.

Others who are in similar situations know what you are going through because they have familiarity with the experience. You emerge from your pain by being with others who healed from their pain.

There is no right or wrong from your experience. It is painful but something else will be given to you instead.

The People in your Life

I ask God:

What will be given to me?

I hear God say:

All of you will experience loss, no one escapes it.

I will fill this void with something new within you, a new understanding of the deeper meaning to your life. Remember that many lives are affected when someone leaves.

No one will take their place but that wasn't the purpose. The purpose was to open your heart and keep it open, wide open. For without it, nothing grows.

Love is like a magic element that you can't get enough of.

I ask God:

What do you mean by that? How can love be an element?

I hear God say:

It is simply elementary my dear one. Go back to grade school as a young one and learn to love simply as a child would. They are so innocent coming into this world and are transformed in the world by what they see and learn. They must know love.

Chapter Six

I ask God:

Are you saying love is the cure all for loss? I just don't get it!

I hear God say:

There is nothing to get but be in the elements of it all, meaning love is all there truly is. There is no permanence in the human form the way you see it and state it. Know this: that it is a form that does not stay or last - it is unrealistic for you to think that the form does not change. What goes on is the love you have for one another - that is what is of value. The value is in the meaning to how lives are shaped and formed by love.

I ask God:

When you say the elements, what do you mean?

I hear God say:

I mean elementary as in school. Are you schooled in love or was that not your teaching? Who were your instructors and what did they teach when you were growing up? An element is an ingredient that is necessary and instrumental to your understanding of me. I love no one until they come to me is utter and pure nonsense. I see all and know all -- I am God. I know that often you act like school children wanting to have your way with things when my way is to have you know love.

The People in your Life

I ask God:

What if my loss and circumstances are more than I can endure?

I hear God say:

How do you handle yourself when things get difficult? What do you gain from the situation you are placed in? There is nothing to endure. Life is meant to be appreciated.

When things happen that upset you to your core, do you realize that there is more than one way to look at something or someone? Permanent attachments to people may hinder you when they leave for you feel you are lost without them. It is not for you to despair but to appreciate the times you have together. For now you will both move on. Nothing is lost or gained; it is just an emotional state of being that you are left with. Choose wisely your thoughts and feelings for they will remain with you till you depart. Remember to get back into the dance of life.

I say:

Since it is only a temporary stay here, none of this big stuff should weigh me down. Now I think I get it.

I hear God say:

You are getting there but in a roundabout way.

Chapter Six

Even though I have experienced loss in my life, one of the best ways to recover is to give to another. Give to someone you know or to a stranger. When you give it is called a blessing. You can be a blessing. How? Do something for someone expecting nothing in return. Be a blessing in their life. You can do that in so many ways: offer a ride to someone, pick up their groceries, and mow their lawn….give back!

Ask yourself...

    101. Who have I blessed this week and how?

_____
_____
_____
_____

Ask yourself...

    102. Who in my life do I feel blessed by and why?

_____
_____
_____
_____

FORGIVENESS

Forgiveness has a powerful impact on getting you past anger and resentment. If you learn to forgive, you can transcend your anger and mend your relationships. When someone presses your buttons or makes you angry it is often your own unresolved issues that cause your negative feelings.

Anger has this nasty way of getting inside of you and when it does it can take hold of you and even affect you physically. For much of my life I was angry with my Dad due to his drinking and abuse. I shut him out. The end result was that I shut myself down as well. His death was a gift to me because I had a supernatural encounter when he passed that brought me closer to God.

Had I not had that supernatural encounter, who knows when I would have come to know God or myself? I am so grateful for that encounter but knowing what I know now, I wish I had forgiven my Dad and spent time with him while he was alive.

Anger ties into so many different feelings. When I feel unloved, I often get angry. I fight for so many of the wrong reasons. Sometimes I fight just to prove that I am right. This is how I am? Wrong!!! I can be mindful of my behavior and myself at all times. I need to begin to identify what is provoking me in the first place. I can also learn not to make excuses for my bad behavior but work on fixing myself.

I ask God:

Where was I headed when I was so angry?

Chapter Six

I hear God say:

In a downward spiral. Think of yourself like a slinky. Be amenable with what is and isn't. The journey is not perfect, but you are perfectly made in the holiest of forms. You are a person who is here on self-discovery. The self-discovery is simply this: you are put to the test many times but you will keep on repeating it if you can't change your answers.

The answer to life is not so mysterious. It is simply this: love yourself, as you love your life. You are an active participant and player in the field of the lands. The lands are limitless. Know no limits. You may have disappointments, but they will fade away as time heals all. Disappointments are different for each of us but without these experiences you are not who you are.

I ask God:

What about forgiveness, God? Why was I so stubborn to forgive my Dad?

The People in your Life

I hear God say:

Don't be so hard on yourself my dear one. There was much abuse. You didn't understand the role you took on to be a compassionate and caring woman evolving one step at a time. You managed to confess your misgivings and heal from this and you now see your relationships in a whole new light. Some people who are wounded come across your path, but forgive them regardless of what you feel their injustices might be. While everyone moves in different directions on their own paths, all roads eventually come to me. There isn't anything that I cannot heal. <u>How you deal with one another is important</u>. I use the word "deal" because all are dealt hands they must learn to play. They must learn to play well for in the end all the cards will be placed in a pile. There are no winners with war, anger, rage, savage behavior, it is beneath mankind to avenge, kill and destroy.

I ask God:

So how do we handle blow-ups and inappropriate behavior?

Chapter Six

I hear God say:

With love, discipline, and honoring the divinity in each one of you. There is a light inside all, but it grows dim for some. They have never known a loving touch; touch them with your love. Though they must pay a price for their actions, all is forgiven. Jesus died on the cross and all was forgiven. He rose for mankind to see the illumination of the king, the Holy one known as God. He walked on water, was spat upon, and took no revenge against those he loved - his disciples, whom he taught while he was here. He came back to them where they stood. They now must face the consequences of their actions or inactions. We must all face our consequences. There is no justice in beheading someone; that behavior is obscene. An eye for an eye and the world goes blind; Gandhi knew that far too well. Peace is the holiest form of Me in action. Take this action and you will know my will and ways for my people.

Wow, God can forgive anything, so why can't I forgive someone the way He does? Am I too proud or stubborn or hurt that I won't budge off my anger or dismiss any grudge I hold against someone?

I ask God:

Does this mean I must take them back and be in an active relationship with them?

I hear God say:

Only if you choose. Love isn't being with someone. Love is found in your heart. In other words love is expressed and carried deep within you. You can't see it - often it can be illusionary. It is how you feel. How do you feel?

I ask God:

"I feel disappointed or like it never happened as if they've disappeared from my life."

I hear God say:

Interesting, Cindy! As if it has never happened means you have gotten over your pain and moved on. When you wipe the slate clean and can honestly look back and not be riled, you have mastered the emotion of forgiveness.

Forgiveness is also a gift to give yourself. By releasing your pain you set yourself free. When you no longer carry ill will or flare up at the mention of another person's name, a sense of peace and calmness will come over you and you will wish the same for them.

With each new relationship comes a new start. Beginnings are for everyone. A birth or a death is about life. Life is a cycle, a regeneration of thoughts, ideas, and knowledge. We seem at times to lack compassion for others. We need to understand that people are affected by our attitudes. But, more importantly, I am affected by my own attitude.

Ask yourself...

    103. Make a list of all the people that you think require your forgiveness.

_____

_____

Chapter Six

Ask yourself...

    104. Make a list of all the people you want to forgive you and the reasons.

___

___

___

___

Ask yourself...

    105. Make a list of all your regrets and transgressions. Ask yourself if you can forgive yourself for what you have on your list.

___

___

___

___

Ask yourself...

    106. Which of my attitudes that affect others am I least proud of?

___

___

___

___

The People in your Life

Communicate

Chapter Six

Habits   *The Old Cindy*

I didn't spend a lot of time with people who were important to me. I didn't talk about love. I didn't feel blessed and often I felt nothing. I spent a lot of time talking about meaningless stuff.

Discoveries

I would let anyone into my life. I went to a lot of my husband's softball games, even though I wasn't a sports fan. I would hang out, drink beer, and party every Sunday after the game. My husband managed his life around the games. They were such a huge part of our life. Many of the people who were in my life were friends of my husband. I didn't enjoy the activities he liked, but if I didn't participate in them I would hardly see him. I resented being left alone all the time as he disappeared and went to so many sporting events. I did not know what it was truly like to be in a marriage relationship since ours felt like such a failure. There was no intimacy, romance or deep conversation; we weren't each other's best friend.

Spiritual Revelation

I didn't understand the purpose of people being in my life and what they were teaching me or how and what I was teaching them. I did not know the significance or meaning of unconditional love.

Habits

I now figure out who I want to spend time with and why. I look at the people God has put in my path and sense what it is we are supposed to do. I ask if there is something for us to do to serve God. It's a big world out there, yet I seem to attract new people around me. I reflect upon who I attract into my life and what we are being shown and taught from our relationship. I learn all the time from all of my relationships. I welcome the time I have to spend in all relationships and value the time and the people I spend it with. Even though some relationships do not turn out the way I thought they would, I still appreciate the experience.

Discoveries

I finally know what it is to be in an intimate relationship and really share things. I express myself when it comes to things I hold in my heart and I now can say "I love you" to someone. I welcome talks about sensitive subjects to gain a deeper understanding of one other. I have many types of relationships in my life - friends, business partners, future husband, brother, and more. I discern and pray about my relationships and learn all the time from each of them. I believe in being in a marriage with a Spiritual partner, it is a key part of the relationship.

At the end of my life I would like to have people at my funeral whose lives I have touched deeply. I hope these relationships were filled with an exchange of love and compassion for one another, with memories of time we spent together and no regrets.

Spiritual Revelation

I was taught unconditional love even though it was hard to learn. I finally understood it and felt it. I am grateful to have love cross my path and realize the significance of it. Love is such a powerful and wonderful emotion. I also know God loves me; no matter what, for His love is unending.

Chapter Six

After reading Cindy's transformation from the "Old Cindy" to the "New Cindy", please turn to chapter 13 and complete your evaluation of the "Old You". Allow at least 21 days after finishing the workbook, and then complete the "New You" section.

Remember *change is a process.* Like many things in life, *progress takes time.*

»»»»» Take Action «««««
Choose at least one action you can take now.

- Say I love you to someone this week.
- Be kind to someone you have been mean or indifferent to.
- Tell someone why you appreciate them in your life.
- Ask someone how you affect them positively and negatively.
- Do something nice for someone you know, and expect nothing in return.
- Do something nice for someone you don't know, and expect nothing in return.
- Write an apology letter to yourself about something you have been unable to forgive yourself for.

Chapter 7

Do I Dress My Part?

*The fashion that never goes out of style
is knowing that I am so worthwhile.*

Chapter Seven

In This Chapter	➢ How do you feel about fashion? ➢ Do you judge people by appearance? ➢ Do you behave a certain way based on how you dress?

We live in a visual world. How we judge someone or how we are judged is often based on our appearance and the way we are dressed.

What do clothes and appearance say about us? Do they impart an image that we want to convey to others? Are they an expression of who we really are? How does our appearance affect our relationships? Do the roles we play in life – friend, mother, teacher, lover, etc. - affect how we dress?

JUDGMENT
Ask yourself...

107. Do I judge a person by the way they dress? Does my opinion change after getting to know the person I've judged or is my first impression usually accurate? Explain.

_____
_____
_____
_____

Do I Dress My Part?

Ask yourself...

    108. How do I feel when I am being judged by my dress/appearance?

___
___
___
___

Ask yourself...

    109. If I see a person with unusual dress/appearance do I judge them?

___
___
___
___

Ask yourself...

    110. Does my dress affect how I feel about myself? Explain.

___
___
___
___

Chapter Seven

Ask yourself...

    111. Do I think I need to look a certain way?

___

Ask yourself...

    112. Do I pay attention to what is fashionable? Why?

___

Ask yourself...

    113. If I went to a party wearing jeans when everyone else was wearing a fancy outfit, how would I feel?

Ask yourself...

    114. If someone spills wine on my clothes at a party, how would I react? Would my night be ruined?

___

APPEARANCE

As we age, our hair may turn gray: it has for me. I have chosen to stop fighting Mother Nature by dying my hair, which was consuming 3 hours out of my life every 6 weeks. I also was somewhat proud of the wisdom that I was learning to display. I realized that beauty is not based on appearance, but comes from deep within. I now see beauty beneath the surface. I appreciate it. I recognize it and, more importantly, I see and feel it in myself and others. I realize beauty doesn't diminish with age.

There were times I have wanted bigger breasts and skinnier thighs. While you always seem to want what you don't have, I am at the point of being content with what I do have. I can lose weight or color my hair, but the core feelings deep inside of me are how I dress myself. I have asked God to help me with those feelings. I know I am dressed in a garment that is always visible, namely me.

Ask yourself...

    115. Do I feel I have to be young and attractive to be of value?

Chapter Seven

Ask yourself...

116. Give an example of someone who is old and is valued.

_____
_____
_____
_____

I hear God say:

If you are hung up on your dress and appearance just "be." No matter how you look, maybe you are not appreciating the real beauty that lies within you. You are a prized possession

Make over

Chapter Seven

Habits   *The Old Cindy*

I didn't care about fashion for how I dressed wasn't a priority in my life. Often I would have my hair done to please my husband. I would ask him how he would like my hair to look, sacrificing how I would like to wear my hair. I would try to save money by not going to the beauty salon and instead dying my hair myself. As a result, I had many shades of color including green, bleached blonde, and orange.

Discoveries

I didn't care about fashion. I really didn't enjoy it. I didn't care if I wasn't wearing the latest fashion. I wasn't hung up on the way I looked for it wasn't important to me. I got married wearing huaraches sandals (if you can remember what they even were), not a bride's typical pair of wedding shoes!

Spiritual Revelation

I made surface judgments about people and their appearance and I would wind up being deceived by them. They were not who I thought they were. I let them into my life without knowing who they really were. I would be nice to someone based on what they had and owned versus who they were. It didn't even matter if I liked them or not.

Habits

The New Cindy

I feel good inside no matter what I wear and I have fun picking out and selecting what outfit to wear. I don't worry if someone else doesn't like it; I like it and that is what matters. I dress to please myself. I do what I want with my hair for there is no bad hair day, just a bad attitude. I choose what I feel when it comes to looking at me. I treat myself to the beauty salon and enjoy the time I spend there. It feels like I am on a mini retreat. The beauty salon is an item in my budget.

Discoveries

I love to shop for bargains. I rummage through the stores looking for creative and inexpensive ways to duplicate a style or look that I've liked in a magazine or on a TV show. I discovered my love of fashion and design - now I love creating outfits. I also love to recycle and wear vintage items. When I get married I will wear pumps - goodbye huaraches!

Spiritual Revelation

I don't judge a person by how they look or dress. I talk to everyone and try to get to know them before deciding whether I want them in my inner circle. I take my time and see a person's patterns and behaviors so I don't get caught off guard and unaware of how they really are. I use discernment as best I can.

I often go to the person who is being avoided in a room or crowd, sensing what it must be like to be ignored. I don't like people being left out or excluded; I find it to be hurtful. We do not pick our appearances, we are born with them. There is beauty in everything and everyone - you just have to be open to seeing it.

Chapter Seven

After reading Cindy's transformation from the "Old Cindy" to the "New Cindy", please turn to chapter 13 and complete your evaluation of the "Old You". Allow at least 21 days after finishing the workbook, and then complete the "New You" section.

Remember *change is a process*. Like many things in life, *progress takes time*.

»»»»» Take Action «««««
Choose at least one action you can take now.

- ➢ Start a conversation with a person who you would never talk to because of the way they are dressed or the way they look.
- ➢ Go to an event and talk to a person whose dress clearly does not fit the occasion.
- ➢ Get dressed up in your best duds and go to a casual event. Observe other people's reactions.

Chapter 8

Not Another Workshop Or Book

I will read and study to no avail,
if what I learn does not prevail.

Chapter Eight

In This Chapter	➢ Why so many books and why should I bother to read any of them? ➢ What do you gain by attending workshops? ➢ What's all this new stuff that comes along and does it work?

Not another workshop! Not another book! That is how I feel at times. Just when I think I've heard it all, something new comes along. Is there something we need to learn or hear again? Why? We retain what we hear or what we read depending on our emotional state and our willingness to learn. It takes effort to attend a workshop, read a book and be fully present to what you are about to learn. But isn't it worth spending the time to learn?

I ask God:

God, what do you think of books?

Not Another Workshop or Book

> I hear God say:
>
> *They are healing, they are therapeutic they are gems of peoples lives put together on a page that share many precious moments and many personal matters. They are a guide to living a perfect life. They are energy, they are art. They are works that are passed on. They are endeavors of mankind. They are history, they are knowledge, and they are to be used for the right purpose. They are a way of communicating across the spans of time and place. They need to be read.*

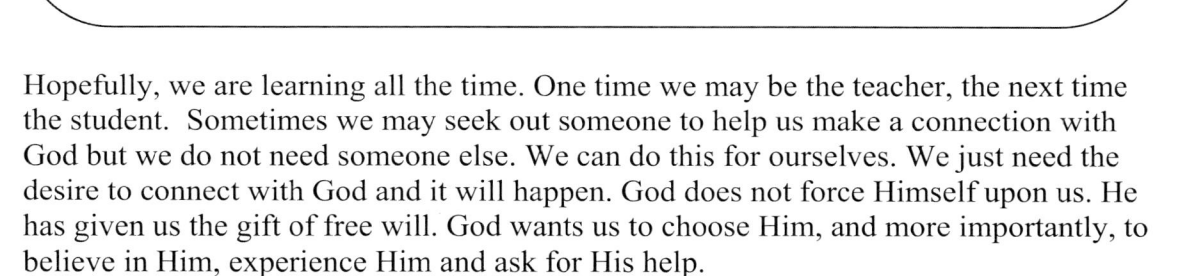

Hopefully, we are learning all the time. One time we may be the teacher, the next time the student. Sometimes we may seek out someone to help us make a connection with God but we do not need someone else. We can do this for ourselves. We just need the desire to connect with God and it will happen. God does not force Himself upon us. He has given us the gift of free will. God wants us to choose Him, and more importantly, to believe in Him, experience Him and ask for His help.

I am the light, I am the light bulb: I just need to know what to plug into. Please check out the facilitators and healers you work with. What are they about? It is important that the facilitator does not take credit for the healing. The facilitator is only the vehicle through which the Holy Spirit works. It is the Holy Spirit that comes from God who does the healing. It is the union of light and love that heals us through the holy Trinity - the Father, Son and Holy Spirit.

I love to watch Spirit at work. I welcome it. I can never get enough of it. I also know that we learn exactly what it is we need to learn from a teacher, workshop or book. Your Spirit has a way of taking in what is important to you at that time.

A mind can be opened or closed to new ideas. The point is we need to be willing to listen and learn. I have come to the conclusion that we never stop learning. Learning new things is what keeps us growing. As we learn new concepts and gain new perspectives we may change our own personal point of view for the better.

Chapter Eight

If you keep hearing about a book or a class, time and time again, it is God telling you something. God speaks to you through others. Pay attention to that. God works in extraordinary ways. While we all relate to things differently, God knows how to work with each one of us individually. When I am seeking His help, it appears. You need to take an active role in your life. Participate! All of our learning doesn't come from books and classes. Our life experiences, if we learn from them, give us a degree all in itself.

Have I said enough about learning? There can never be enough said about learning. There is so much to learn that we must be careful not to over think, for over thinking can often talk us out of something we know intuitively. I use my heart now to feel life instead of just thinking life. I am aware that there is a difference between what you think and what you feel. You may, for example be able to describe what love is but do you feel it in your life? You may not be able to see the sun's rays on your skin on a summer afternoon, but you do feel the warmth it generates.

It is important to apply in your life those lessons learned. We need to work on ourselves. Remember to thank God for being patient with us while we work on improving ourselves.

When I don't get it or I feel blocked and am unable to change my thought that is the time I need to pray for help. Prayer is my pipeline to God. So even with all the books and workshops, we still need to pray. I pray every morning when I wake up and before I go to sleep at night. If you want to change your life, pray.

Study

Chapter Eight

Habits *The Old Cindy*

I rarely attended church and when I did, I did not enjoy it. You would not find me at a lecture/workshop that did not interest me, and my interests did not include topics such as how to find happiness or improving self love or getting to know oneself and others more..

Discoveries

I would not attend any type of self help, spiritual or healing workshop. I did attend business related seminars and conventions. Since reading was not a priority, I didn't take time to read and I did not have favorite authors or books. How sad when I look back.

Spiritual Revelation

I didn't think it was important to learn anything new. What would I study anyway since I didn't have a clue who I was or what I liked. School was a chore and so I avoided it. I never considered reading the Bible for it seemed boring. I didn't know what I could learn from it and even if I did read it, I didn't think I would understand it.

Habits   *The New Cindy*

I now make it a point to go to classes to learn something new. I either attend a weekly spiritual related group or class or participate in some related community event. I love to attend praise and worship concerts as singing to God takes me to another zone where I dance and move with God. I love to hear and share stories of God's role in our lives with others. I don't cram God down anyone's throat but when asked, or if I feel I should share something, I talk about what God is doing or has done in my life. I also would love to hear what He is doing in your life. If I hear about a book or class over and over again I will look into taking or reading what is constantly being shared with me.

Discoveries

I love to learn and I attend classes and workshops whenever I can. I love to learn about a wide variety of subjects. I read books that I feel called to read and I look forward to reading them. I get so much pleasure from classes. I get a great deal of pleasure from what I learn as well as the interaction while sharing with new and familiar faces. I teach classes and I treasure the emotional reactions from students whose lives are touched deeply in my classes.

Spiritual Revelation

I have learned the importance of learning and I realize that learning never stops. You are never too old to learn. I value knowledge. I have taken Bible classes and love them. I wanted to read the Bible and learn from the stories. I do all I can to learn more about myself and God. I also have been told by many that I have a unique way of teaching self discovery. The messages I receive from God and share with others reveal new perspectives about their lives. It is so wonderful a feeling to share such private spiritual and emotional moments with people. I see clearly that we all are God's children, one family under His love.

Chapter Eight

After reading Cindy's transformation from the "Old Cindy" to the "New Cindy", please turn to chapter 13 and complete your evaluation of the "Old You". Allow at least 21 days after finishing the workbook, and then complete the "New You" section.

Remember *change is a process*. Like many things in life, *progress takes time*.

»»»»» Take Action «««««
Choose at least one action you can take now.

- Within the next 7 days, read a book relating to a physical, emotional, or spiritual topic.
- Within the next 3 months, attend a workshop or lecture or community shared event.
- Share with someone something that you found interesting from a workshop or a book you read.

Chapter 9

Prayers and Signs from God

I have found the place I dare to dream. It is all within my means.

Chapter Nine

> **In This Chapter**
> - How to receive clarity from the Universe.
> - How to pray and receive a sign from God.
> - How you can effectively change your life through prayer.

Prayer is one of the ways I communicate with God. I pray every night before I go to sleep. I pray every morning when I wake up. I pray when I walk, when I'm in the shower, on the grocery line, and when I'm driving. I love to pray.

I ask God each day to fill me with joy in my heart, knowing that this is the day that God has made and that I have a lot to be thankful for. My prayers always include a "thank you" to God; I am so grateful for His guidance. He is my confidante, my inspiration, and He has helped me rise above every situation that has occurred in my life.

I have experienced first-hand the power of prayer. It has changed my life; it can change yours. Prayer gives you clarity, about yourself and about the Universe. It speeds up learning and puts things into action.

I have witnessed and heard many things that prayer has accomplished for others – from the mundane (like finding a parking place) to the joyful (like getting engaged) to the miraculous (like healing cancer).

Prayer is not always about asking God to provide answers to your problems or to solve difficult situations that you are facing. A prayer can be asking God for something as simple as helping me appreciate that today was a wonderful day.

One day I encountered a young boy who was blind; he was accompanied by a man and a woman. I was caught off-guard when I heard God say, "You need to pray for this boy." Although I was in a hurry, I did as God asked. I approached the boy, asked him his name, and told him that God had asked me to pray for him and I was wondering if that would be okay. He didn't get a chance to answer; the man he was with was obviously angry and told me I was interfering with the boy's lesson. I apologized, quietly told him that God had asked me to pray for the boy and I began to pray. The man took the boy by the arm and scurried off. I was confused and upset by his refusal to accept my prayer and God's help and I drove back home in tears.

I asked God for clarity and began to see what I couldn't see before.

> God said:
>
> *You have shown great courage in doing as I asked. By trusting in me, without knowing the reason or the outcome of my request, you have shown your loyalty and commitment to serving me and you have opened up the pathway to knowledge and insight.*

He was right! I would never, without God's request, have walked up to someone and asked if I could pray for him. That took courage; for me it was a bold act. My emotional reaction to the man's rejection forced me to look at my feelings in a new light. I learned that in doing God's will I have to be open and willing to accept other peoples' feelings and that, although I may not understand the immediate purpose of God's requests, I know He is guiding me to new heights and helping me to discover my whole being, my purpose and my spiritual path.

And so I pray. Here is an example of one of my daily prayers

MY PRAYER TO GOD
*I thank you God for your knowledge.
Your knowledge is contained inside of me
for you are always there.
Help me to remember to call on you each day
knowing you listen and care.
May my words and thoughts
both conscious and subconscious
be filled with your wisdom.
May my heart feel your love.
May I express your love.
May I see things as you need me to see them.
Thank you for bestowing upon me my life.
Thy will be done.
Written by Cindy Miller ©*

Chapter Nine

You can decide to pray to God as I do. The choice is yours, of course, but I promise you that your life will change if you open yourself up to God. You can pray anywhere and anytime. You will grow; you will move forward, and you will see clearly what you haven't been able to see before. Pray and see what He has in store for you.

Make up your own prayer to God. Say your prayer twice a day and continue to say the same prayer until you know it by heart. Start each day with that same prayer. Say other prayers (conversations) with God to get in the habit of praying. Remember a prayer is just a conversation with Him and after all, you talk with your friends and loved ones, so why not Him?

_____

_____

_____

_____

_____

_____

_____

_____

I have found that keeping a prayer journal is helpful. I keep one and I write not only my prayers but also God's answers. We sometimes forget how God has answered our prayers, especially when times are difficult, chaotic and stressful. When you look back at your prayer journal, you will be reminded of all the times God has worked things out for you, even when you thought He wasn't listening. Remember that God is always with you, but how and when he answers your prayers is up to Him. He may not answer you immediately, but if you are patient and open to receiving His answers, He WILL answer you, when and where He pleases.

SIGNS

God may not always answer your prayers with words. He can also talk to you through signs. When I pray and do not hear an answer to my prayer, I ask God to show me a sign.

Whenever I see a rainbow, I know it is a sign from God. As with many of God's signs, rainbows often appear out of nowhere. To me a rainbow is truly a symbol of the magnificence of God and it is His way of reaching out to me.

I experienced the miracle of God's presence once when I hosted a piano concert. The pianist I'd hired was a friend of mine, but we were having difficulties in our relationship. The first song he played was "Somewhere Over the Rainbow" which was not on the schedule and he had no plans to perform it. He told me later that he simply felt "compelled to play it". He didn't know it then but he was being used by God to mend our relationship. God understood what needed to be done and I understood God's sign. This was a powerful experience for me and I recognized how powerful God was in healing me. By allowing myself to be open to Him to see what He was telling me through his signs, I received a wonderful healing that day.

When I pray and do not hear an answer to my prayer, I ask God for a sign. I ask my question and then ask God to show me a physical sign. Here is how it works: I select an item that is something I normally would not see and ask God to show it to me.

Here is an example:
There was a person who was in and out of my life. Because of the many issues between us, I needed to know if I should still connect with him. I asked God to show me an elephant within the next three days as confirmation to move forward with this relationship. The elephant was the sign I was asking God to show me. Next, my brother Steve invited me to spend the weekend on a farm. I love spending time with my brother so I immediately accepted his invitation.

I went to the farm for the weekend and couldn't believe what I saw! As I was walking the farm grounds I came across a life size bronze statue of an elephant. I stood there shaking my head, looking at the elephant, remembering my request to God to show me a sign. I had presented God with this unusual request and He showed me the sign. What's the odds of seeing a full size elephant?

Chapter Nine

This prayer request has worked for me, time and time again. I have shared this prayer request idea with others and guess what; it worked for them as well. It is amazing! I don't know why God answers us the way He does, He just does. I may not always like the answer, but I trust it and am not afraid of it.

God is the architect of my life. I try to understand the reasons why things turn out the way they do. When I do not understand, I know God has it all under control. I just need to trust Him. I will never be given all the answers, but I also know He holds the best plans for my life. I ask Him to fill me with wisdom and insight so that I may understand the fullness of who I am in Him and to understand beyond my current understanding. I also know that I am important to God and that He is my Father. God loves and cares about me like no one else possibly could. He loves each one of us that way. God's love is endless; it never goes away. God will always love each and every one of us. His love for me is unconditional as it is for you too.

Signs can help you figure out relationships.

Have you ever noticed when you look back at your life that signs were given to you?

Ask yourself...

    117. What signs have you noticed? What were they?

_____

_____

_____

_____

Ask God to give you a sign about something that you are struggling with.

Make sure you give a time frame and see what develops.

Prayers and Signs from God

Write about it and be sure to thank God for answering you.

Chapter Nine

Habits

The Old Cindy

I did not pray for signs to be shown to me for as far as I was concerned, I was all alone. I would get way too attached to someone for the wrong reasons, often not making a good choice when I did. I didn't know love and went after the wrong type of love.

Discoveries

I had no idea what a Spiritual sign was or what to do when I was in a difficult situation. I would get upset and stay upset. I would hold on to anger and stay upset. There was a period of time when I would not eat, sleep or function the way I should because I was so upset about a relationship. I did not understand loss and had no idea where you go when you died.

Spiritual Revelation

I didn't know God would provide signs, so I never asked or noticed them. I was unaware of my heavenly helpers or supernatural encounters and didn't experience one until I was at my lowest point. I had to break down emotionally to have God get my attention. He did so with a supernatural experience, which led to such a huge revelation for me that it altered my life permanently

Habits   *The New Cindy*

I don't chase anything now. I let things come to me when they are supposed to. I make requests to God about my life and know He has it under control with His divine timing. I love being amazed over and over again by how God works with me and cares about every aspect of my life. I know we have been given the gift of free will and that we are able to choose. I now choose to live a Spiritual life.

Discoveries

I know how to recognize a Spiritual sign and how to ask for one. I can be upset but not to the point of not functioning. I may not like what has happened but I know it will lead to healing and that a greater good will unfold. I remain as positive as possible.

Spiritual Revelation

I know to pray, talk and ask God for direction in every area of my life. I also know God speaks through people. This is another way I can receive messages when I am seeking an answer. Things magically occur in my path which I know are heaven sent. Many times I have asked God if He wants me doing sessions with people and a new client will call that same day to schedule a session. I realize that was an answer from God. I am being heard and watched out for by God each day. He puts things in my path all the time. I work on staying aware to recognize what He is showing me.

Chapter Nine

After reading Cindy's transformation from the "Old Cindy" to the "New Cindy", please turn to chapter 13 and complete your evaluation of the "Old You". Allow at least 21 days after finishing the workbook, and then complete the "New You" section.

Remember *change is a process*. Like many things in life, *progress takes time*.

»»»»» Take Action «««««
Choose at least one action you can take now.

- In the next three days write a prayer about something you would like to change in your life. Thank God for taking care of this.
- Ask God to show you a sign or give you a message to some question you need answered, specify a time frame.
- Find a person with whom you can pray together about something.

Chapter 10

We All Have This In Common

No one escapes dying so why can't I just spend my time flying high until it is time to say goodbye?

Chapter Ten

In This Chapter	➢ Do we have anything in common? ➢ When I depart, have I lived my life well? ➢ Have I made amends with who I need to before I depart? ➢ What do you appreciate about life? ➢ What do you need to change inside to feel your life's grandeur?

We all have this in common. We will all die. I like to say "cross over." No one escapes this event. It will be an event that will touch many if we have lived our life right.

When we die we return home. We land in a place where there is no beginning and no end. I envision heaven with gardens galore, sunshine, everyone is nice, there is no crime, there is no……. etc. Can there be two heavens - the life hereafter and the life here too? There is so much beauty here that it is hard to fathom even more beauty. But hold on a minute! Can't we experience heaven on earth, right here, right now? Of course we can, but what prevents us from doing so?

Ask yourself...

> 118. Do I sense the beauty here on earth? Name what is beautiful about the planet.

_____
_____
_____
_____

Ask yourself...

119. Do I sometimes forget that awesome sense of appreciation for my life? What do I appreciate about my life?

_____
_____
_____
_____

Ask yourself...

120. What makes what might seem like an ordinary day extraordinary?

_____
_____
_____
_____

Ask yourself...

121. If my day wasn't extraordinary, what ruined it for me?

_____
_____
_____
_____

Chapter Ten

Ask yourself...

122. What are the problems I complain about? How can I change them?

_____
_____
_____
_____

Ask yourself...

123. Do I find small things to cherish every day? What was the last little thing I cherished?

_____
_____
_____
_____

Ask yourself...

124. Is there something in me that needs to change in order to feel God's presence in everything, including me?

_____
_____
_____
_____

Ask yourself...

    125. What do I feel proud of? Do I let pride get in my way?

___

Ask yourself...

    126. What will make me feel that I have lived a good life when I depart this world?

___

Ask yourself...

    127. Was my time here meaningful to me? How so?

___

Eventually the curtain comes down on all of us, and sometimes with an encore. While some feel satisfied, others feel they have had enough. I have heard some say, "You can

Chapter Ten

take me. I'm ready to go" or "I don't want to leave, I'm having a good life" or "I am afraid to go." There are so many thoughts about this.

In A Christmas Carol, Ebenezer Scrooge learned the meaning of generosity, kindness and love through the ghosts of Christmas: Past, Present, and Future. Scrooge was shown the inside scoop as he looked at his life from a bystander's viewpoint. He witnessed what happened through the years and realized how he could have changed his life by changing his thoughts and actions.

Like Scrooge, I too am always working on transforming myself. I choose to live my life and apply what I now know to my remaining time. I choose to be more generous, kind and loving. It has taken me a while to learn all of this. I want to buy the biggest goose, just like Scrooge did, and celebrate my life. The story ends with God blessing everyone.

I say:

I think I've got it now!

I hear God say:

Not so fast! There is still a little more.

Believe in God

Chapter Ten

Habits   *The Old Cindy*

I did not feel any day was extraordinary. I did not keep a gratitude journal for what was there to be grateful for? I would never consider having a journal or writing about my life or thoughts. I would not put pen to paper or evaluate or take inventory on anything in my life.

Discoveries

I didn't think I had much in common with anyone. I didn't fit in. When I was with people, I felt like an outsider looking in at everyone from a distance. I did not realize how special I was. I was not grateful for the day and never thought that this day could be my last.

Spiritual Revelation

I never took time to understand people or think about what they may be going through in their lives. I didn't understand their behavior so I would complain a lot, never seeing just how negative I was.

162

Habits

The New Cindy

I am now writing this book and loving it. I love to write. I love to share. It gives me joy to reach out to someone while sharing my experiences of what I have learned. There is so much to share as we all learn from each other as we deal with the many difficult things we experience throughout our lives. I like to share lessons on how we heal from life's struggles to reach a place of joy! I also like to write with twinges of humor; laughter is so healing.

Discoveries

I am grateful for life and realize how precious it is. I know that time is so valuable because you don't get it back and you don't know how much future time you will have. You only have the present moment. That is why it is a present.

We will all depart from this earth plane and it is important to me that I know God for He and heaven are where my permanent home is. I choose to know Him while I am here for I do not want to be a stranger to Him but a well-received friend whom He welcomes back when I go to heaven.

Spiritual Revelation

I look, feel and sense people and can actually feel their pain. I cry with them, laugh and hear about their lives and do what I can to reach out to them. I welcome the opportunity to be of service to others. I also know when not to overextend and what is mine to do and what is Gods. I mentioned surrendering and I mention it again - it is up to me to surrender to God so I can witness what He can do.

Chapter Ten

After reading Cindy's transformation from the "Old Cindy" to the "New Cindy", please turn to chapter 13 and complete your evaluation of the "Old You". Allow at least 21 days after finishing the workbook, and then complete the "New You" section.

Remember *change is a process.* Like many things in life, *progress takes time.*

»»»»» Take Action «««««
Choose at least one action you can take now.

➢ Go for a walk and find ten things that are beautiful.
➢ Tell the person you complain to the most five things about them that are wonderful.
➢ Find someone who is opposite of you and discover what you have in common.

Chapter 11

Let Go, Let In

Let go of all you love,
Throw your cares in a pile
And just smile.

Chapter Eleven

> **In This Chapter**
> - Are you ready to throw out material possessions?
> - Do you see how letting go certain relationships can improve your life?
> - What do you gain when you give something away?

Try packing away everything you own but be aware it may feel as though you are giving up your entire life. My brother renovated his apartment and gave away everything he owned. The result was he felt free. Think of the transformation that occurs when you give everything away.

So what now? He gave away everything and he was left with nothing, no not quite. Months later my brother's apartment was the nicest it has ever been. There was opulence and elegance to the newly created space. What he thought was a nice space before had now turned into an even nicer space. Let go – let in!

Now I was renovating my home and my brother and his friend stopped over for a visit. My brother wanted me to get rid of a lot of my stuff. Letting go of my stuff overwhelmed me for I thought it was still useful. Yeah, right! Maybe others need to let go but certainly not me. As I thought about my things, I wondered why they were so important to me. My brother's friend commented that my brother and I had the same problem holding on to stuff. His friend is good at letting go; he does it naturally. He also has a high prosperity consciousness. His ability to let go ties into his core beliefs and viewpoints on prosperity and lifestyle. His lifestyle is filled with elegance and opulence. He never worries about replacing anything. He believes in a God who provides abundance for us all.

They advised me what to keep and what to buy. They insisted it had to be new not used. I had enough old stuff around me. The first thing that had to go was my sofa, so we went online and searched for sofas and I found one I liked. We relaxed and watched TV and as I flipped through the channels I found an evangelist speaking on planting a seed in your life. He said that when you let go and give it to God you have surrendered the outcome to God. God wants us to rely on Him. We also do not need to stockpile junk for a rainy day. How can God replace what we give up if we do not release it to Him? Do we give God the chance of showing us He is God? We need to know that self-sustaining is not up to us alone.

Coincidentally, the evangelist mentioned that a new sofa would cost $1,000 and he asked "don't we need more than a sofa in our life"? If only we realize that God wants more for our life than we can possibly imagine. So I went into action and bought the sofa. After all, I spend a lot of time on it, ha ha. What better place to begin the lesson of letting go. I would also like to point out that not only did my brother and his friend have to convince me but so did the evangelist who was shouting on the TV in the background. God was at work driving home His message to me through so many different means. Guess what? I got it. *Good-bye old sofa, hello new!*

A friend and I were on vacation with a car loaded with his art, music and equipment. At one point I needed to use the car, but he would not allow it. He told me that if something happened to his stuff while I used the car it would be disastrous. His whole life was in his vehicle. He was extremely adamant about this.

Do you believe his whole life was in his vehicle like he thought? Can't canvas, paintbrushes and cameras be replaced? If we lose material items does that mean we no longer have a life? If we are stripped away of physical stuff, isn't there still a lot left? After all, do we like who we profess ourselves to be? Do we know we are worth so much more than all of our stuff?

Not only is there the stuff to let go of, but we also hold on to and cling to people, situations and dreams when we would be better off letting go of them. We can use **let go** and **let in** with so many of the scenarios we play out in our life. I may have to let go of a best friend but a new best friend will arrive if I keep my heart open to all the possibilities that life is bringing my way. Like the ocean whose waves ebb and flow, having such beauty, when I look out at it, my life can be beautiful just like an ocean wave. Something rolls in, something rolls out, I am part of the process. So I let go of what I love, stay loving, and see what rolls in on the next wave. I don't feel as if I am waiting, I keep my balance; I ride, get knocked off now and then but get back up and surf all the way to the shore with a smile on my face, exclaiming "I did it"! As I walk, sometimes things get swept ashore and come back to me, for I know this is truly meant to be.

Chapter Eleven

Ask yourself...

    128. What will you let go of?

_____
_____
_____
_____

Ask yourself...

    129. Who will you let go of?

_____
_____
_____
_____

Realize that you are *a treasure just as you are*. Say out loud:
- ❑ I am an active participant in my life.
- ❑ I am mindful of my state of being.
- ❑ I am in control of my feelings and thoughts.
- ❑ I trust the Universe will bring in what I need.

Let Go, Let In

I ask God:

In my life's journey, what do I need to let in?

I hear God say:

Let me be a part of your life. I am willing to win your heart. My love for you is eternal.

I will continue to discover and uncover myself as I play the game of life. I will see you out there with me. When we meet, may we recognize one another from the soles on our feet, oh I mean the souls that we are.

Hey I'm a girl, so when it comes to shoes I have many pairs. It is time to get comfortable wearing new shoes. Let go of the old and let God bring in the new. Here's to both of us walking in a pair of new shoes. While our soles take us on a wonderful path may our souls experience a wonderful journey. I walk in mine. You walk in yours. We both walk with God. Praise God and a big Amen!!!!!!

I ask God:

Are we done yet?

I hear God say:

There is still one more thing.

Chapter Eleven

Habits *The Old Cindy*

I would control everything and never let go. I did not want to give up control. If I controlled the situation I would be happy or at least that's what I convinced myself of.

Discoveries

I did not let go; I wanted to be in charge. I was a control freak and didn't trust my outcome to anyone else, including God. I would not ask God to help me with someone or something that was precious to me; I figured that I could do it better. I would not even ask friends, for I trusted no one.

Spiritual Revelation

I fought tooth and nail to be in control of life. I loved being at the helm and making everyone do as I wanted them to do. I didn't understand that I had a choice to let go and let God! I didn't understand that God was abundant and offered the generosity of the Universe. I did not believe things would come back to you if you let go of control and gave them to God.

Let Go, Let In

Habits

The New Cindy

I now "let go and let God". When I take it back I give it back and ask God to take over. I do not want to solve it but move past it and focus on God and myself. I realize you cannot serve man and God at the same time. If I keep my focus on God, all will go according to His plan and I will feel His peace and contentment within me.

Discoveries

I now give to God what I love most, myself. I believe when I turn problems over to Him, He will take care of it. He knows how hard it is for me to let go and give up someone or something I want. I know God can solve what I can't. So I turn it over to Him and wait for an answer. I choose not to feel as though I am waiting. I appreciate being in the moment and staying there. I don't want to make my life be about one person or stuff. I choose to make my life be about God.

Spiritual Revelation

I understand that God is limitless and can heal and give us new beginnings. I can give up the old and let in the new in so many different areas of my life. Each day here is a miracle and I am part of that miracle. I have been given another day to explore life. It is up to me how I greet each day on my exploration.

Chapter Eleven

After reading Cindy's transformation from the "Old Cindy" to the "New Cindy", please turn to chapter 13 and complete your evaluation of the "Old You". Allow at least 21 days after finishing the workbook, then complete the "New You" section.

Remember *change is a process.* Like many things in life, *progress takes time.*

»»»» Take Action ««««
Choose at least one action you can take now.

➢ Give something away that you have been unable to part with.
➢ Buy yourself something new.
➢ Fill a garbage bag and throw it out today.

Chapter 12

I Know Who I Am

I travel with God's blessing wherever I go,
His divine knowledge I need to know!

Chapter Twelve

In This Chapter
- How has your relationship with God changed?
- Understanding who you really are.
- What my new choices are now.

I am coming to a close on sharing what I have learned so far in my life. My life is about me but not in a selfish way. It all comes from within. My source is God. He lives inside of my heart. He lives in your heart too.

We can be loving or selfish, erratic or calm, close or distant, quiet or talkative, and we can cry and show our feelings or hide them from others. It is up to each one of us to decide what it is we really want. You decide. You do not have to earn anything to make your decision. You profess yourself to be who you truly are and what you believe in. Your truth is your truth and that is important, for it represents who you are.

The lessons in your life are yours to do with what you wish. If you feel you have been served lemons, then make lemonade; swig it down and drink again. If you do not think lemonade is delicious, then drink something else. The well only looks dry if you allow it to. When you view something your eyes perceive what you wish to see. Perception is in the eyes of the beholder, so change your perception and your life will change

I hope you got something out of reading **IS THAT ALL THERE IS...*the journey within*.** It is my truest desire that you do. You finished this whole journal, and answered a lot of questions during this journey. Now please reaffirm by saying out loud:

1. I choose to be happy.
2. I will be joyful.
3. I will focus on better habits.
4. I will have hopes and dreams.
5. I will not focus on life's drama.
6. I will develop positive relationships with the people in my life.
7. I will dress my part.
8. I will continue to learn.
9. I will know and experience love.
10. I will remember there is beauty here on earth.

11. I will let go and let God.
12. I realize I am a treasure just as I am.

The truth is always there to be discovered. Our time here is so brief; may we all make the most of it.

Perhaps the first thing on your list may be for you to take a long sleep. The prayer goes *"If I die before I wake I pray the Lord my soul to take."* Oh, I've got this now. He's going to take me. He takes the good, the bad and the ugly. He has an **insatiable** love for each one of us.

Do you fully believe in Him?
Do you believe in yourself?
Do you now know how important it is to truly love yourself?

I welcome God and I wind up …………..

Saying …
"I FINALLY KNOW WHO I AM!!!"

I hear God say:

She's got it!

You do too. Shucks………………..
GOD DOESN'T HAVE ANY FAVORITES!

Your relationship with God and yourself awaits you.

Amen

Chapter Twelve

PS
As for me, I'm going to continue to write inspirational books, as I feel led. God will lead me, and He will lead you too. I hope you continue to read **our** work. I call it **our** work because it is all divinely inspired. I ask for God's help and He is there, always was, always will be.

Believe in yourself

Chapter Twelve

Habits   **The Old Cindy**

I didn't know who I was. I didn't take the time to know myself. I didn't take time to know God. No one ever helped me to look inside to discover who I was.

Discoveries

I was raised a Catholic and religion seemed very ritualistic to me.
I never looked for or knew truth about God.
God was not important to me.
God did not feel like a part of my life.
God was not my Father.

Spiritual Revelation

I didn't realize much about anything when it came to Spiritual matters or teachings. I didn't want to be taught about it either; it didn't interest me. I felt as if I was wasting my time at church.

I Know Who I Am

Habits   *The New Cindy*

I know me. I love me. I love God. I know myself a little more each and every day. I remain true to myself, I remain true to God. Guess what? I love me! I love God! Amen!

Discoveries

I know the truth I stand for is within me on a very deep level.
I know God. I know so much more about me.
I enjoy attending churches. Each congregation has something to teach me and I them.
I ask God what church I should go to.
I have conversations with others of different religions about God.
I do not like separation of people for we are all one under God.
My friends represent many different religions and beliefs.
It doesn't dissuade me what your religion is. I know who I am.
I know religion is not the only way to connect with God.
God is the most important part of my life.
God will always be a part of my life.

Spiritual Revelation

I have so much more to learn about the gifts I have been given by God. I incorporate as much as I can into living a spiritual life, being aware of God and myself - physically, emotionally and Spiritually. I ask God where He wants me to go to church. He always tells me to visit many congregations and share my light with others. I now dedicate a portion of my life scheduling healing events to help others. I love doing it too.

Chapter Twelve

After reading Cindy's transformation from the "Old Cindy" to the "New Cindy", please turn to chapter 13 and complete your evaluation of the "Old You". Allow at least 21 days after finishing the workbook, and then complete the "New You" section.

Remember *change is a process.* Like many things in life, *progress takes time.*

You have crossed the finish line ...
Congratulations!
Job well done.

Chapter 13

R U Changing - Transformation

Draw what you would like. What does the new you look like?

***I am a work in Him. I am the song He sings.
Let freedom ring.***

In This Chapter	➢ **Record the Old You as you begin to track and notice your transformation to the New You.** ➢ **Write about the New You when at least 21 days have passed from reading and answering the questions throughout this book.**

Well you finished the book and time has passed. Your healing is underway. Just as a good recipe has different ingredients we have many ingredients in our life too.

Write down what it is you see and notice in yourself and what in your life has changed. Recognize what you are still working on, and where you are, and where you are headed. But stay in the present moment of appreciating who you are today.

The awareness that is inside of you never goes away; you just need to be willing to pay attention to it. That built-in radar I call your intuition is like a G.P.S., which will guide you to where you need to go, so don't worry, you are well on your way. You won't get off your path and, if you do, you can be rerouted. Like the voice on your G.P.S. that tells you "recalculating" you will hear the voice of God inside you each and every day talk to you. Trust in God and your inner knowing. Remain focused on positive thoughts.

Each chapter in this book has a few key moments in my life so that you see the changes I made and where I am today.

I meet each day with a sense and feeling of hope, joy, peace and love along with a deeper understanding of myself.

So begin to write and be proud of the transformation you are making!!!

Write a review of yourself from each chapter:

Celebrate

Chapter 2 - That Thing Called Joy

Your Habits *The Old You*

Your Discoveries

Spiritual Revelation

That Thing Called Joy

Your Habits   **The New You**

Your Discoveries

Spiritual Revelation

Chapter 3 - What Needs to Change?

Your Habits   *The Old You*

Your Discoveries

Spiritual Revelation

What Needs to Change?

Your Habits *The New You*

Your Discoveries

Spiritual Revelation

Chapter 4 - My Aspirations

Your Habits **The Old You**

Your Discoveries

Spiritual Revelation

My Aspirations

Your Habits

The New You

Your Discoveries

Spiritual Revelation

Chapter 5 - The Drama - Is It Holding Me Back?

Your Habits *The Old You*

Your Discoveries

Spiritual Revelation

The Drama - Is It Holding Me Back?
Your Habits

The New You

Your Discoveries

Spiritual Revelation

Chapter 6 - The People in your Life

Your Habits　　　　　　　　　　　　　　　　　　　　　　　**The Old You**

Your Discoveries

Spiritual Revelation

The People in your Life
Your Habits

The New You

Your Discoveries

Spiritual Revelation

Chapter 7 - Do I Dress My Part?

Your Habits　　　　　　　　　　　　　　　　　　　　　　　　　　　　　　*The Old You*

Your Discoveries

Spiritual Revelation

Do I Dress My Part?
Your Habits | *The New You*

Your Discoveries

Spiritual Revelation

Chapter 8 - Not Another Workshop or Book

Your Habits *The Old You*

Your Discoveries

Spiritual Revelation

Not Another Workshop or Book

Your Habits *The New You*

Your Discoveries

Spiritual Revelation

Chapter 9 - Prayers and Signs from God

Your Habits   *The Old You*

Your Discoveries

Spiritual Revelation

Prayers and Signs from God

Your Habits

The New You

Your Discoveries

Spiritual Revelation

Chapter 10 - We All Have This In Common

Your Habits   **The Old You**

Your Discoveries

Spiritual Revelation

I Know Who I Am

We All Have This In Common

Your Habits

The New You

Your Discoveries

Spiritual Revelation

Chapter 11 - Let Go, Let In

Your Habits　　　　　　　　　　　　　　　　　　　　　　　　**The Old You**

Your Discoveries

Spiritual Revelation

Let Go, Let In

Your Habits

The New You

Your Discoveries

Spiritual Revelation

Chapter 12 - I Know Who I Am

Your Habits   **The Old You**

Your Discoveries

Spiritual Revelation

I Know Who I Am

Your Habits

The New You

Your Discoveries

Spiritual Revelation

Personal Notes

Personal Notes

Personal Notes

Personal Notes

About the Author

I am a girl who lives in the country, loves the city, ocean, gardening, hiking, dancing, good food and having fun! I also am serious about my relationship with God which led me to become the founder of a nonprofit for mind, body and Spirit. I write poetry, enjoy music, write inspirational articles, teach, laugh, study holistic and Spiritual teachings, attend group and love people.

My journey is going too fast, as weeks turn into months and the years go by. I cherish the time I have here and who I spend it with. Knowledge is key for me when it comes to the bigger picture and the meaning to my life. I start my day in prayer and at the end of the day close in prayer. I appreciate my life.

You now know a little bit about who I am and I feel enough has been said about me. The o thing I want to close with is JOY! Joy is often the missing and secret ingredient contained i life. It was missing in mine but I found it, I discovered it is always there; it never goes away It is stored up inside of you. You can tap into it immediately. I choose joy now! There is jo in loving me! Amen.